# A Theology of Wonder

# A Theology of Wonder

## G. K. Chesterton's Response to Nihilism

Brian P. Gillen

GRACEWING

First published in England in 2015
by
Gracewing
2 Southern Avenue
Leominster
Herefordshire HR6 0QF
United Kingdom
www.gracewing.co.uk

The right of Brian P. Gillen to be identified
as the author of this work has been asserted in accordance
with the Copyright, Designs and Patents Act 1988.

ISBN 978 085244 855 7

Typeset by Gracewing

Cover design by Michael O'Leary

*He who can no longer pause to wonder and stand rapt in awe is as good as dead; his eyes are closed.*

**Albert Einstein**

# CONTENTS

# ACKNOWLEDGEMENTS

HERE ARE ALMOST too many people to thank who assisted in the completion of this work: Great friends like Kevin Allen, John Burgess, Ilene Biberstein, Mike Geraghty and James Michael Neas who, at times, believed in the project more than I did. I would especially like to thank Fr. Paul Murray, not only for his invaluable insight and encouragement, but for never allowing me to give up on the project. Very special thanks also to Michael O'Leary for the original design of the cover of this book.

I am hugely grateful to my good friend, Fr. John McGuire, for putting me up after 'Sandy'. Great thanks also to my uncle Pat, a true Chestertonian, and my dear aunt Patricia for a lifetime of support.

In a most special way I would like to thank my brother Kevin Gabriel who never pressured for a finish and my sister Eileen who quite often did. Both offered unwavering support and assistance and I am deeply indebted to their contributions that were beyond measure.

This work is dedicated to my mother Bridget Gillen. Her fervent prayers can only be likened to the woman in Scripture who relentlessly petitioned the judge.

# INTRODUCTION

N HIS BOOK *Illustrissimi*, Pope John Paul I addresses a letter to G. K. Chesterton in which he responds to the surprisingly confident conviction of certain modern 'theologians of secularization' that God is dead. 'My dear Chesterton,' he writes, 'you and I do indeed fall on our knees, but before a God who is more alive than ever.'[1] In this letter the Pontiff joyfully aligns himself with Chesterton's theological perspective, and applauds his persistent battle against some of the most life-denying philosophies of modernity. Chesterton is not, of course, an official or professional theologian, but he is nevertheless what we might call a lay theologian. 'With Chesterton,' Étienne Gilson remarks, 'more than literature is at stake … we value him most of all as a theologian.'[2] Writing about Chesterton's celebrated work on St Thomas Aquinas, Gilson went so far as to declare: 'I consider it as being without possible comparison the best book ever written on St Thomas. Nothing short of genius can account for such an achievement.'[3] Other leading Thomists and theologians were no less fulsome in their praise, among them Jacques Maritain, and Anton Pegis. But in what sense exactly is it accurate to speak of Chesterton as a theologian?

In recent years new and helpful light has been cast on the life and work of this great Englishman. Aidan Nichols's book, *G. K. Chesterton: Theologian*, for example, illuminates key structures in his work, highlighting in particular five areas of theological importance:

'Chesterton's argument for the existence of God, his theological anthropology, his Christology, his moral theology and his ecclesiology—or, more widely, his overall sense of the Catholic Church and her faith.'[4] One way to bring into focus the specific genius of Chesterton's theological vision is to examine closely the way he chose to respond to one of the most insidious philosophies of modernity: nihilism. Helmut Thielicke sums up the teaching of this dark vision of life in one brief sentence: 'Nihilism literally has only one truth to declare, namely, that ultimately Nothingness prevails and the world is meaningless.'[5]

The first person to use the term 'nihilism' was Friedrich Heinrich Jacobi (1743–1819), but the nihilist movement as such made its first appearance not in Germany but in Russia in the 1860's. Popularized by the Russian author, Ivan Turgenev, the term 'nihilism' was eventually adopted by a group of disaffected Russians who did not hesitate to declare that all existing forms of society were wholly unacceptable, and must be destroyed. Friedrich Nietzsche, the German philosopher, has been identified in a particular way with the phenomenon of nihilism. His relation to it, however, was decidedly complex. He appeared at times not unaware of the danger it represented but, at other times, appeared as one of its greatest proponents.

In the present study my intention is to show how Chesterton's approach to the mystery of life, and to the great mystery of Being, is the antithesis of nihilism, and how his 'theology of wonder' acts as a brilliant antidote to ward off the negative impact of this philosophy. What will become clear is that Chesterton, as an author, does indeed possess a distinctly lay theology, and it is a theology, a vision, which responds with both the bright intelligence of a mind alive, and with the wonderful innocence of a healed imagination, to what is most lacking in modern thought. In the chapters which follow, my intention is to allow, as much as possible, Chesterton to speak for himself. No commentator can ever hope to measure up to the wit and wisdom of G. K. I make no apology, therefore, for the many quotations from a body of work which is as wonderfully sane and down-to-earth as it is profound and visionary.

## Notes

1    Pope John Paul I, *Illustrissimi: Letters from Pope John Paul I* (Boston: Little, Brown and Company, 1978), 17.

2    Étienne Gilson, 'Letter from Étienne Gilson from the Pontifical Institute of Mediaeval Studies to Fr. Kevin Scannell', *The Chesterton Review* XVIII, no. 2 (May 1992), 53.

3    Étienne Gilson, cited in Maisie Ward, *Gilbert Keith Chesterton* (Lanham: Rowman & Littlefield Publishers, 2006), 146.

4    Aidan Nichols, *G. K. Chesterton, Theologian* (Manchester: Sophia Institute Press, 2009), ix.

5    Helmut Thielicke, *Nihilism, Its Origin and Nature: with a Christian Answer* (London: Routledge & Kegan Paul, 1969), 27.

# CHAPTER 1

# NIHILISM

*There is no other world. Nor even this one. What, then, is there? The inner smile provoked in us by the patent nonexistence of both.*

E. M. Cioran

IHILISM, THE WORD, derives from the Latin *'nihil'* meaning nothing. The motivation behind a great deal of G. K. Chesterton's writing lies in a determined opposition to what is at nihilism's core, namely the conviction that all existence and all human life, therefore, all forms of human culture and civilization, all beliefs and morals, are empty of purpose and meaning. What Chesterton offers us is not simply a cogent denial of nihilism. Yes, there is a brilliantly conceived response to some of the most negative aspects of nihilism. But what is fascinating to observe, over and over again in Chesterton's writing, is the way he is able to lay bare the gigantic lie at the heart of nihilism, relying not on dogged, persuasive argument merely, but on the authority of imagination and on the simplicity of truth found in myths and fairy tales. Chesterton, at his ordinary best, is at least as much a poet as a philosopher.

## I. The Venom of Nihilism

Chesterton knew at first hand the sting of the venom of nihilism. He knew in terrifying depth, therefore, something of the sense of hopelessness and despair that it

brings. This happened when he was a student at the
Slade School of Art in London. Michael Ffinchs, referring to this dynamic and yet deeply unhappy period in
Chesterton's life, remarks: 'While his fellow students
did not want to be discursive and philosophical, Chesterton's mind was moving at an amazing pace, but in
the wrong direction.'[1] Chesterton himself explains:

> I deal here with the darkest and most difficult
> part of my task; the period of youth which is
> full of doubts and morbidities and temptations;
> and which, though in my case mainly subjec-
> tive, has left in my mind for ever a certitude
> upon the objective solidity of Sin ...

> But I am not proud of believing in the Devil. To
> put it more correctly, I am not proud of
> knowing the Devil. I made his acquaintance by
> my own fault; and followed it up along lines
> which, had they been followed further, might
> have led me to devil-worship or the devil
> knows what ...

> In the time of which I write it was also a very
> negative and even nihilistic philosophy. And
> though I never accepted it altogether, it threw
> a shadow over my mind and made me feel that
> the most profitable and worthy ideas were, as
> it were on the defensive ...

> And as with mental, so with moral extremes.
> There is something truly menacing in the
> thought of how quickly I could imagine the
> maddest, when I had never committed the
> mildest crime. Something may have been due
> to the atmosphere of the Decadents, and their
> perpetual hints of the luxurious horrors of
> paganism; but I am not disposed to dwell much
> on that defence; I suspect I manufactured most

of my morbidities for myself. But anyhow, it is true that there was a time when I had reached that condition of moral anarchy within, in which a man says, in the words of Wilde, that 'Atys with the blood-stained knife were better than the thing I am'. I have never indeed felt the faintest temptation to the particular madness of Wilde; but I could at this time imagine the worst and wildest disproportions and distortions of more normal passions; the point is that the whole mood was overpowered and oppressed with a sort of congestion of imagination. As Bunyan, in his morbid period, described himself as prompted to utter blasphemies, I had an overpowering impulse to record or draw horrible ideas and images; plunging in deeper and deeper as in a blind spiritual suicide.[2]

It is worth investigating certain occurrences in Chesterton's life that led to this 'blind spiritual suicide.' Kevin Belmonte points out in *Defiant Joy* that, 'It was at the Slade School that he experienced a period of desolation unlike any he would ever know. It was his dark night of the soul.'[3] The young Chesterton was, for the first time, away from all of his friends and family and now subject to, as William Oddie defined it, 'Current trends in art.'[4] These trends included the cultural licentiousness and cynicism associated with nihilism that was prevalent in London in the 1890s. George P. Landow[5] further explains that, 'The assumptions underlying much of the poetry, fiction, and art of this time centered on an anti-Romantic belief in original sin and in fallen man and nature; the omnipresence of evil and the grotesque; lack of health, balance, and innocence.'[6] The mood and tone of this period was marked by a philosophical ethos of 'Ennui,

incompleteness, a sense of loss, exile and isolation.'[7]
The predominant goal or theme of artistic endeavors
was that of 'Incomplete and unsuccessful attempts to
escape the human condition by means of posing,
artifice, and evil, all of which are conceived of as
unnatural and therefore better than nature.'[8]

Chesterton eventually became aware of the dangers
involved in abandoning the helm of the imagination
to other forces; philosophical or otherwise. Speculating
on how he had allowed his mind to become so dark-
ened, he states that, 'The very fact that I indulged in it
without reason and without result, that I did not come
to any conclusion, or really even try to come to any
conclusion, illustrates the fact that this is a period of
life in which the mind is merely dreaming and drifting;
and often drifting onto very dangerous rocks.'[9] Chesterton avoids catastrophe, however, and does not crash
into those 'dangerous rocks'. He navigates a philosophical maneuver that pits itself against the lure of
nihilism. In his autobiography he explains, 'I have
always had a weakness for arguing with anybody; and
this involved all that contemporary nihilism against
which I was then in revolt.'[10]

K. Dwarakanath reveals the dynamics produced by
Chesterton's grappling with nihilistic culture. His
mind had indeed wandered into some dark places but
his escape from these inner dungeons is where the real
adventure begins:

> Here is a strange and bewildering case of a
> youth who is plumbing the depth of the inner
> moral world, who emerged not as a pessimist
> but as a cheerful romantic. It happens some-
> times that the greater the power of the enemy,
> the greater will be the zeal of those who fight

against him. As the evil appeared to be more and more real and hideous, the zeal to recoil from, and revolt against it became intense, and Chesterton heroically emerged out of the nightmare with a unique experience that gave him a philosophy which was his own. The vitality and excitement of this revolt endured throughout his life, to the wonder and thrill of which he was now more alive than ever.[11]

Victor Frankl, while not commenting on Chesterton directly, does illustrate the direction his mind eventually took. It is a direction that moves outward to the world and others. It is a mind free from the dull and constrained perspective of self:

By declaring that man is responsible and must actualize the potential meaning of his life, I wish to stress that the true meaning of life is to be discovered in the world rather than within the man or his own psyche, as though it were a closed system ...

Being human always points, and is directed, to something or someone, other than oneself—be it a meaning to fulfill or another human being to encounter. The more one forgets himself—by giving himself to a cause to serve or another person to love—the more human he is and the more he actualizes himself.[12]

Chesterton encountered the 'venom of nihilism' as a young man and it was this experience that forever altered his approach to reality. Afterwards, he began to see more clearly the importance of the responsibility to make proper use of one's mind and imagination. It was a distorted use of Chesterton's imagination that had permitted him exploration into such dark depths.

It was his imagination also, however, that enabled him to elevate his mind to proper vision. When the imagination works continually inward, it becomes ensnared and restricted within the narrow confines of the ego. It is within these confines that false abstractions of reality can be encountered as real. It is in the arena of the imagination where the 'venom of nihilism' can deliver its most poisonous sting.

This is perhaps why Chesterton forever appreciated the mind's relationship to what is actually real. This appreciation can be seen while he details the philosophical mechanics of St. Thomas Aquinas's mind in relation to reality. He explains that, 'In the subjectivist, the pressure of the world forces the imagination inwards. In the thomist, the energy of the mind forces the imagination outwards because the images it seeks are real things. All their romance and glamour, so to speak, lies in the fact that they are real things.'[13] Dorothy Sayers, who was deeply influenced by Chesterton, comments on this directional movement of the imagination in *Mind of the Maker*: The creative Imagination works outward steadily increasing the gap between the visioned and the actual.[14] In observing a purpose at work in Chesterton's writings against nihilism, it is beneficial to note that a point-for-point rebuttal is not always being made. Chesterton openly acknowledges his refutation of nihilism but his writings are more of a general literary response to the prevalent nihilistic influences in philosophy and culture. He was responding, in his day, to nihilism as its insidious infiltration was broadening: 'The heresies that have attacked human happiness in my time have all been variations of either presumption or despair; which in the controversies of modern culture are called optimism and pessimism. And if I wanted to write an autobiography in a sentence (and I hope I shall never write a longer one), I should say that my literary life has lasted from a time when men were losing happiness by despair to a time when they are losing it by presumption.'[15] Chesterton demonstrates throughout his writings how nihilism begins in presumption and ends in despair but he doesn't make a mere denial of nihilism. He reveals that the very opposite of nihilism is what is most true: 'At the back of our brains, so to speak, there was a forgotten blaze or burst of astonishment at our own existence. The object of the artistic and spiritual life was to dig for this submerged sunrise of wonder.'[16]

Chesterton, while often encouraging the imagination, is never substituting it for reason. He strongly defends reason by attacking some of the most egregious assumptions of nihilism, particularly with regard to human thought. If thought itself is to be questioned as unreal, man no longer has a philosophical point of reference. Once reason is dismissed, nihilism may have its way. As exciting as some nihilistic presumptions first appear, it soon becomes apparent just how well paved, with good intentions, the road to hell actually is. Once man has pulled the rug of reason out from under him he has no foundation on which to stand. He is now cut adrift and floats towards those 'dangerous rocks':

> [I have observed] that what peril of morbidity there is for man comes rather from his reason than his imagination. It was not meant to attack the authority of reason; rather it is the ultimate purpose to defend it. For it needs defence. The whole modern world is at war with reason; and

the tower already reels. For there is a great and possible peril to the human mind: a peril as practical as burglary. That peril is that the human intellect is free to destroy itself. Just as one generation could prevent the very existence of the next generation, by all entering a monastery or jumping into the sea, so one set of thinkers can in some degree prevent further thinking by teaching the next generation that there is no validity in any human thought. It is idle to talk always of the alternative of reason and faith. Reason is itself a matter of faith. It is an act of faith to assert that our thoughts have any relation to reality at all. If you are merely a sceptic, you must sooner or later ask yourself the question, 'Why should anything go right; even observation and deduction? Why should not good logic be as misleading as bad logic? They are both movements in the brain of a bewildered ape?' The young sceptic says, 'I have a right to think for myself.' But the old sceptic, the complete sceptic, says, 'I have no right to think for myself. I have no right to think at all.'[17]

Nihilism perceives any traditions, religions, or system of beliefs, relating to the divine as completely lacking in objective value. In fact, concepts such as 'Objective value' are completely rejected by nihilism, and so the demise into nothingness must be accelerated. As Henry T. Edmondson states, 'Nihilism is, in a sense, worse even than atheism: the atheist is content to disbelieve, whereas, the nihilist must "destroy God" and every vestige of his memory.'[18]

Chesterton had a keen sense as to where certain philosophies would lead, especially those that offered a false sense of liberation. He understood that Friedrich Nietzsche was a significant supporter of certain aspects

of nihilism, in particular of those facets of the philosophy that do away with God and conventional morals,
preferring a new world order directed by those who
are both daring and bold enough to brandish their
unyielding 'Will to power.' There lies a great irony,
however, hidden from those who presume to take
possession of reality by force of will. Chesterton
exposes Nietzsche's motives quite simply:

> Nietzsche imagined he was rebelling against
> ancient morality; as a matter of fact he was only
> rebelling against recent morality, against the
> half-baked imprudence of the utilitarians and
> the materialists. He thought he was rebelling
> against Christianity; curiously enough he was
> rebelling solely against the special enemies of
> Christianity, against Herbert Spencer and Mr.
> Edward Clodd. Historic Christianity has always
> believed in the valor of St. Michael riding in
> front of the Church Militant; and in an ultimate
> and absolute pleasure, not direct or utilitarian,
> the intoxication of the spirit, the wine of the
> blood of God.[19]

Chesterton was saddened by how easily men could be
seduced by nihilism. He had grappled with it first
hand and consequently, approached those who had
fallen under its spell with compassion. While writing
about his friend George Bernard Shaw, Chesterton
seeks to pinpoint exactly what had attracted him to
Nietzsche. In his book on Shaw, Chesterton laments:

There are indeed doctrines of Nietzsche that are not
Christian, but then, by an entertaining coincidence,
they are also not true. His hatred of pity is not Christian, but that was not his doctrine but his disease.
Invalids are often hard on invalids. And there is
another doctrine of his that is not Christianity, and also

(by the same laughable accident) not common sense; and it is most pathetic circumstance that this was the one doctrine which caught the eye of Shaw and captured him. He was not influenced at all by the morbid attack on mercy. It would require more than ten thousand mad Polish professors to make Bernard Shaw anything but a generous and compassionate man. But it is certainly a nuisance that the one Nietzsche doctrine which attracted him was not the one Nietzsche doctrine that is human and rectifying. Nietzsche might really have done some good if he had taught Bernard Shaw to draw a sword, to drink wine, or even to dance. But he only succeeded in putting into his head a new superstition, which bids fair to be the chief superstition of the dark ages which are possibly in front of us- I mean the superstition of what is called the Superman.[20]

The idea of a superman is basically this: We as human beings are evolving from one stage to the next, pushed forward by an unstoppable force towards our destiny. Judeo-Christian morals were part of that stage which is now past and no longer serves a purpose. To cling to this past stage is futile. One must embrace the Superman and accept the future or be compromised by what cannot be stopped. The idea of a superman who has evolved past Judeo-Christian concepts of good and evil rests on an enormous presumption of self. In a conversation about people 'Who believe in themselves' Chesterton had this to say, 'Shall I tell you where the men are who believe most in themselves? For I can tell you. I know of men who believe in themselves more colossally than Napoleon or Caesar. I know where flames the fixed star of certainty and success. I can guide you to the thrones of the Super-

men. The men who really believe in themselves are all
in lunatic asylums.'[21] To the core of this philosophy,
which had seduced many of his contemporaries,
Chesterton poses the following questions:

> In one of his least convincing phrases, Nietzsche
> had said that just as the ape ultimately pro-
> duced the man, so should we ultimately
> produce something higher than the man. The
> immediate answer, of course, is sufficiently
> obvious: the ape did not worry about the man,
> so why should we worry about the Superman?
> If this Superman will come by natural selection,
> may we leave it to natural selection? If the
> Superman will come by human selection, what
> sort of Superman are we to select? If he is
> simply to be more just, more brave, or more
> merciful, then Zarathustra sinks into a Sunday
> school teacher; the only way we can work for it
> is to be more just, more brave, and more merci-
> ful; sensible advice, but hardly startling. If he is
> to be anything else than this, why should we
> desire him, or what else are we to desire? These
> questions have been many times asked of the
> Nietzsche-ites, and none of the Nietzsche-ites
> has even attempted to answer them.[22]

The 'venom of nihilism' flourishes and takes hold
wherever pride resides and perhaps it was intellectual
pride that had seduced Shaw and others. In the wake
of nihilism, reason and logic prove to be of little use.
Chesterton's questions remained ignored and unan-
swered. John R. Betz points out, 'That the power of
rhetoric often eclipses the power of thought in the
history of philosophy and theology is no surprise,
especially after Nietzsche, when one can dispense with
all pretensions to the contrary; when the most elabo-

rate systems of thought no longer manifest the "cunning of reason" in its world-historical adventure, but simply various brute assertions of the will to power.'[23] Chesterton is absolutely unimpressed with Nietzsche's superman and his 'will to power'. He writes:

> To be in the weakest camp is to be in the strongest school. Nor can I imagine anything that would do humanity more good than the advent of a race of Supermen, for them to fight like dragons. If the Superman is better than we, of course we need not fight him; but in that case, why not call him a Saint? But if he is merely stronger (whether physically, mentally, or morally stronger, I do not care a farthing), then he ought to have to reckon with us at least for all the strength we have. If we are weaker than he, that is no reason why we should be weaker than ourselves. If we are not tall enough to touch the giant's knees, that is no reason why we should become shorter by falling on our own.[24]

Intelligence, like the imagination, is also susceptible to false directional movements. When not striving towards authentic reality, intelligence risks the perils inherent in nihilism. The intellect is now open to believing in Nietzsche's superman or the aspirations of Nazi Germany. Intellectual pride darkens and fogs the mind, tempting it to consider the unreal. Nihilism adds to and validates prideful delusions. What spared Chesterton from this 'fog of unreality' was his humility. He never presumed to fully understand anything or anyone. For Chesterton a blade of grass was a miraculous event and a human being, a profound mystery, to be approached with reverence and humility.

Chesterton was in some sense prophesizing the horrors that were to come during World War II and beyond. Shaw and others could not see such evil. They were caught deep within the spell of nihilism. Chesterton did not know details of how the Nazis would attempt to implement Nietzsche's superman, but he knew well the dangers of such a philosophy. Peter Kreeft points out that, 'Nietzsche was not only the favorite philosopher of Nazi Germany, he is the favorite philosopher of hell ... Like Nazism, Nietzsche may scare the hell out of us and help save our civilization or even our souls by turning us away in terror before it's too late.'[25] Chesterton, during his time, was sounding the alarm against nihilism. According to Quentin Lauer:

> Had Chesterton lived to see what the Nazi 'supermen' were to make of this kind of breeding, his attacks might have been even more violent than they were, but the fight would be the same fight—against those who think that the ability to bring about change is equivalent to the capacity to make the moral judgment as to what changes are desirable. Once again we can see that action unaccompanied by profound moral thinking runs a serious risk of being evil.[26]

Chesterton had a gift for seeing into the essence of things and he saw right through nihilism's intellectual temptations. He saw through its false promises of grandeur and might. In fact, he was horrified by the brash reduction of reality made to suit the capricious ego.

Chesterton took no pride in being correct in his assessment of any philosophy and never bullied his opponents with his views. He was, however, always about the business of inviting his opponent to a better way of perceiving reality. Chesterton accepted reality as a gift with great humility. He had the following to say about the intellectual ethos of his day:

> [W]e may say that the most characteristic current philosophies have not only a touch of mania, but a touch of suicidal mania. The mere questioner has knocked his head against the limits of human thought; and cracked it. This is what makes so futile the warnings of the orthodox and the boasts of the advanced about the dangerous boyhood of free thought. What we are looking at is not the boyhood of free thought. It is vain for bishops and pious bigwigs to discuss what dreadful things will happen if wild skepticism runs its course. It has run its course.
>
> The last attempt to evade intellectualism *ends* in intellectualism, and therefore in death. The sortie has failed. The wild worship of lawlessness and the materialist worship of law end in the same void. Nietzsche scales staggering mountains, but he turns up ultimately in Tibet. He sits down beside Tolstoy in the land of nothing and Nirvana. They are both helpless— one because he must not grasp anything, and the other because he must not let go of anything. The Tolstoyan's will is frozen by a Buddhist instinct that all special actions are evil. But the Nietzcheite's will is quite equally frozen by his view that all special actions are good; for if all special actions are good, none of them are special. They stand at the cross-roads, and ones hates all the roads and the other likes all the roads. The result is—well, some things are not hard to calculate. They stand at the cross-roads.[27]

Chesterton never allowed fads or philosophies to dissipate his convictions. All the suffering in the world never tempted him to disbelieve in the foundational goodness of the world. He knew there was always a greater reality present. In *Sir Walter Scott*, he writes: 'The center of every man's existence is a dream. Death, disease, insanity, are merely material accidents, like a toothache or a twisted ankle. That these brutal forces always besiege and often capture the citadel does not prove that they are the citadel.'[28]

## II. The Antidote of Wonder

The procedure for making an antidote for a particular toxin is to inject the toxin into an animal in small doses and the resulting antibodies are extracted from the animal's blood. These anti-venoms are used to treat those attacked by poisonous animals. Metaphorically speaking, G. K. Chesterton was a powerful antidote to the philosophical poisons of his day and still remains a most precious and needed medicine in our own age. Mark Armitage had this to say about Chesterton's approach to life:

> This insistence on the goodness of the created order marks a rejection not only of the pessimism of oriental religions and philosophies but of the kind of world-weary philosophy that was to be developed by Schopenhauer and Nietzsche (among others). For Aquinas and Chesterton philosophy and theology are the 'praise of life' rather than an apology for life, and Chesterton sees what we might term the doxological aspect of Aquinas's metaphysics of wonder as the perfect antidote to the poison of pessimism.[29]

Chesterton's refutation of nihilism happens on many levels. His most philosophical response however, can be seen when he explains the ideas of Aquinas. Considering exactly where all other systems of thought go wrong, Chesterton refers to Aquinas on Being:

Aquinas has affirmed that our first sense of fact is a fact; and he cannot go back on it without falsehood. But when we come to look at the fact or facts, as we know them we observe that they have a rather queer character; which has made many moderns grow strangely and restlessly skeptical about them. For instance, they are largely in a state of change, from being one thing to being another; or their qualities are relative to other things; or they appear to move incessantly; or they appear to vanish entirely. At this point, as I say, many sages lose hold of the first principle of reality, which they would concede at first; and fall back on saying that there is nothing except change; or nothing except comparison; or nothing except flux; or in effect that there is nothing at all. Aquinas turns the whole argument the other way, keeping in line with his first realization of reality. There is no doubt about the being of being, even if it does sometimes look like becoming; that is because what we see is not the fullness of being; or (to continue a sort of colloquial slang) we never see being being as much as it can. Ice is melted into cold water and cold water is heated into hot water; it cannot be all three at once. But this does not make water unreal or even relative; it only means that its being is limited to being one thing at a time. But the fullness of being is everything that it can be; and without it the lesser or approximate forms of being cannot be explained as anything;

unless they are explained away as nothing...
Thus, while most sages come at last to nothing
but naked change, he comes to the ultimate
thing that is unchangeable, because it is all the
other things at once. While they describe a
change which is really a change in nothing, he
describes a changelessness which includes the
changes of everything. Things change because
they are not complete; but their reality can only
be explained as part of something that is complete. It is God.[30]

Chesterton viewed the world through a lens of
wonder. For him, it was the only way to truly see the
world and all that it beholds. This lens of wonder was,
for Chesterton, his most provocative tool against
nihilism. He confronts nihilism by encouraging and
replenishing a sense of wonder into the commonplace
experiences of the day. He accepts with gratitude and
wonder the unmerited gift of life. Rescued by humility,
he stares at reality from a different vantage point. No
longer distorted by his own perceptions, he beholds
everything in wonder by the mere fact that it exists:

When I had been for some time in these, the
darkest depths of the contemporary pessimism,
I had a strong inward impulse to revolt; to
dislodge this incubus or throw off this nightmare. But as I was still thinking the thing out
by myself, with little help from philosophy and
no real help from religion, I invented a rudi-
mentary and makeshift mystical theory of my
own. It was substantially this; that even mere
existence, reduced to its most primary limits,
was extraordinary enough to be exciting. Anything was magnificent as compared with nothing. Even if the very daylight were a dream, it
was a day-dream; it was not a nightmare. The

mere fact that one could wave one's arms and
legs about (or those dubious external objects in
the landscape which were called one's arms and
legs) showed that it had not the mere paralysis
of a nightmare. Or if it was a nightmare, it was
an enjoyable nightmare.[31]

G. K. Chesterton can enjoy a nightmare and it is
important to know why. He is able to apply essential
elements in the works of Saint Thomas Aquinas to
reality. The Saint's valuable metaphysics seems to have
been lost in our neglectful age but do regain their
clarity with Chesterton. Herbert Marshall McLuhan
insightfully compares Chesterton and Aquinas:

> It is time to abandon the literary and journalistic
> Chesterton to such critical fate as may await
> him from future appraisers. And it is also time
> to see him freed from the accidental accretions
> of ephemeral literary mannerisms. That means
> to see him as a master of analogical perception
> and argument who never failed to focus a high
> degree of moral wisdom on the most confused
> issues of our age.[32]

Chesterton refers often to Heavenly realities. He views
this world as a herald to the staggering and wondrous
reality beyond human comprehension. In doing so, he
alludes to our truest nature and asks that we accept
our own mystery with humility. He asks us to 'remember that we forgot.' Then we can cease striving to
define ourselves by an earthly standard and surrender
to something greater than ourselves:

> We have all read in scientific books, and,
> indeed, in all romances, the story of the man
> who has forgotten his name. This man walks
> about the streets and can see and appreciate

everything; only he cannot remember who he
is. Well, every man is that man in the story.
Every man has forgotten who he is. One may
understand the cosmos, but never the ego; the
self is more distant than any star. Thou shalt
love the Lord thy God; but thou shalt not know
thyself. We are all under the same mental
calamity; we have all forgotten our names. We
have all forgotten what we really are. All that
we call common sense and rationality and
practicality and positivism only means that for
certain dead levels of our life we forget that we
have forgotten. All that we call spirit and art
and ecstasy only means that for one awful
instant we remember that we forgot.[33]

Chesterton was infected with the deadly venoms of
his age but was able to produce an anti-venom. He was
now able to act as a metaphysical physician to his
patient; modern man. The antidote takes effect when
one remembers what has been forgotten. In *St. Francis
of Assisi*, Chesterton explains how turning our minds
to the source of all things lends profundity to them:

[A man] sees more of the things themselves
when he sees more of their origin; for their
origin is a part of them and indeed the most
important part of them. Thus, they become
more extraordinary by being explained. He has
more wonder at them but less fear of them; for
a thing is really wonderful when it is significant
and not when it is insignificant.[34]

Chesterton is able, through his sense of wonder to
acknowledge all things as significant. He once
remarked to a reporter, 'From the beginning I think I
was staggered by the stupendous marvel of existence—by the miracle of sunlight coming through a

window, by the miracle of people walking on legs through the streets, by the miracle of people talking to each other.'[35] And again, writing to his fiancée, Frances, he notes: 'I do not think there is anyone who takes quite such fierce pleasure in things being themselves as I do. The startling wetness of water excited and intoxicated me; the fieriness of fire, the steeliness of steel, the unutterable madness of mud. It is just the same with people.'[36]

What the world needs is vision and, in Chesterton's understanding, it is the vision of the saint which is the necessary antidote to false and mistaken ways of thinking such as nihilism. Often saints live their lives in stark contrast to the world around them.

> The Saint is a medicine because he is an anti- dote. Indeed, that is why the saint is often a martyr; he is mistaken for a poison because he is an antidote. He will generally be found restoring the world to sanity by exaggerating whatever the world neglects, which is by no means always the same element in every age.[37]

Chesterton is unquestionably one of the best antidotes to nihilism in our modern age. His acute understanding and application of Thomistic thought allowed him to confront philosophical constructs that were opposed to and contradicted reality. Dale Ahlquist, President of the American Chesterton Society, points out,

> Chesterton argued eloquently against all the trends that eventually took over the twentieth century: mate- rialism, scientific determinism, moral relativism, and spineless agnosticism. He also argued against both socialism and capitalism and showed why they have both been the enemies of freedom and justice in modern society.[38]

## III. *The Argument from Joy*

Chesterton has a gift for shifting perspectives back to reality in a way that is surprisingly joyful. In *The Common Man*, he writes:

> The sentiment of (*A Midsummer Night's Dream*) ... is the mysticism of happiness ... the conception that as man lives upon a borderland he may find himself in the spiritual or supernatural atmosphere, not only through being profoundly sad or meditative, but by being extravagantly happy. The soul might be rapt out of the body in an agony of sorrow, or a trance of ecstasy; but it might also be rapt out of the body in a paroxysm of laughter.[39]

Contemplating the spirituality of St. Francis of Assisi, Chesterton insists upon a distinct relationship that the saint has with nature. It is a relationship that somehow immediately makes sense and we find ourselves saying 'yes' to it right away:

> The main point of Christianity was this: that Nature is not our mother: Nature is our sister. We can be proud of her beauty, since we have the same father; but she has no authority over us; we have to admire, but not to imitate. This gives to the typically Christian pleasure in this earth a strange touch of lightness that is almost frivolity. Nature was a solemn mother to the worshipers of Isis and Cybele. Nature was a solemn mother to Wordsworth or to Emerson. But Nature is not solemn to Francis of Assisi or to George Herbert. To St. Francis, Nature is a sister, and even a younger sister: a little, dancing sister, to be laughed at as well as loved.[40]

Joy for Chesterton is not simply a delightful moment
in time that has been enjoyed. It is an invitation to our
truest nature as human beings. It is a door to eternity.
On the question of joy Nichols writes:

> According to Chesterton, joy as a response to
> being is the principal signal of transcendence
> that human experience offers ... Chesterton
> suggests that the theme of joy, pervasive in his
> writings, indicates a kind of aperture in experi-
> ence: via this aperture we are open to the tran-
> scendent realm that is God. Chesterton speaks
> of it as a kind of rupture in the chain of cause
> and effect that governs the finite universe.[41]

In *The Ballad of the White Horse*, Chesterton uses the
phrase 'joy without cause'.[42] It's a striking phrase, and
it provokes this wise reflection from Nichols:

> It may be said at once that by calling joy
> uncaused, Chesterton did not mean that it was
> a random or chance occurrence, ontologically
> rootless. On the contrary, precisely because, for
> him, joy is neither empirically bounded nor
> ethically relevant, its foundation must be
> sought at a deeper level, where the finite opens
> onto the infinite. Were joy a reaction to empiri-
> cally specific states or situations, it could be
> regarded as determined by those states or
> situations. Were it ethical in content, it could be
> seen as a reflection of a self-constituted human
> meaning. But since, as Chesterton indicates, it
> is neither of these things, its *raison d'être* must
> be sought at a point which may be called
> metaphysical: on the finite-infinite frontier. Joy,
> he argued, lies deeper than happiness or unhap-
> piness, pleasure or pain. All of these are reac-
> tions to particular conditions or events within

existence, whereas joy is the reaction to the fact
that there should be such a thing as existence at
all. Intimately related to wonder before the fact
of being, joy is an implicit affirmation of the
doctrine of creation and hence of the truth of
theism.[43]

Paradoxically, Chesterton encourages one to be serious
about joy and all that is good. In being serious about
goodness we take ourselves less seriously thus allowing a more authentic experience of ourselves:

> By one of those queer associations that nobody
> can ever understand, a large number of people
> have come to think that frivolity has some kind
> of connection with enjoyment. As a matter of
> fact, nobody can really enjoy himself unless he
> is serious. Even those whom we commonly
> regard as belonging to the butterfly classes of
> society really enjoy themselves most at the
> crises of their lives which are potentially tragic.
> Men can only enjoy fundamental things. In
> order to enjoy the lightest and most flying joke
> a man must be rooted in some basic sense of the
> good of things; and the good of things means,
> of course, the seriousness of things. In order to
> enjoy even a *pas de quatre* at a subscription dance
> a man must feel for the moment that the stars
> are dancing to the same tune. In the old reli-
> gions of the world, indeed, people did think
> that the stars were dancing to the tunes of their
> temples; and they danced as no man has danced
> since. But thorough enjoyment, enjoyment that
> has no hesitation, no incidental blight, no
> arrière-pensée, is only possible to the serious
> man. Wine, says the Scripture, maketh glad the
> heart of man, but only of the man who has a

heart. And so also the thing called good spirits is possible only to the spiritual.[44]

Chesterton contends that man is more true to himself when joy is central to his spirit and grief is just a passing mood. Joy, not misery, is man's natural end:

> The mass of men have been forced to be gay about the little things, but sad about the big ones. Nevertheless (I offer my last dogma defiantly) it is not native to man to be so. Man is more himself, man is more manlike, when joy is the fundamental thing in him, and grief the superficial. Melancholy should be an innocent interlude, a tender and fugitive frame of mind; praise should be the permanent pulsation of the soul. Pessimism is at best an emotional half-holiday; joy is the uproarious labour by which all things live…To the modern man the heavens are actually below the earth. The explanation is simple; he is standing on his head; which is a very weak pedestal to stand on. But when he has found his feet again he knows it. Christianity satisfies suddenly and perfectly man's ancestral instinct for being the right way up; satisfies it supremely in this; that by its creed joy becomes something gigantic and sadness something special and small. The vault above us is not deaf because the universe is an idiot; the silence is not the heartless silence of an endless and aimless world. Rather the silence around us is a small and pitiful stillness like the prompt stillness in a sick room. We are perhaps permitted tragedy as a sort of merciful comedy: because the frantic energy of divine things would knock us down like a drunken farce. We can take our own tears more lightly than we could take the tremendous levities of the angels.

So we sit perhaps in a starry chamber of silence,
while the laughter of the heavens is too loud for
us to hear.[45]

What is needed if we are to acquire a Chestertonian
perspective on reality is, perhaps, above all else, the
grace and authority of imagination. It is the vision
imagination offers which serves as the tool to help us
navigate the philosophical pitfalls of modernity. Peter
Kreeft writes:

> Let's use the image of water. A city is sur-
> rounded by walls and it is fighting a war. The
> enemy is trying to knock down the walls, but
> they can't do it because the walls are too strong.
> Then a great rainstorm comes. As the rain
> suddenly gets underneath the walls and softens
> the ground, the walls fall down and the city is
> conquered. Rational arguments are like bullets.
> They're useful, but if we're going to conquer the
> city that is the world, we need rain and not just
> bullets. Images and attractive symbols are like
> the rain. They soften the ground as they seep
> into the unconscious. Lewis called it 'baptizing
> the imagination.'[46]

In *Surprised by Joy* C.S. Lewis acknowledges:

> In reading Chesterton, as in reading MacDon-
> ald, I did not know what I was letting myself in
> for. A young man who wishes to remain a
> sound Atheist cannot be too careful of his
> reading. There are traps everywhere—'Bibles
> laid open, millions of surprises,' as Herbert
> says, 'fine nets and stratagems.' God is, if I may
> say it, very unscrupulous.[47]

Chesterton appeals to both reason and imagination. It
is as if he is speaking to the forgotten child within; the

child who once loved and trusted and perceived love
as commonplace. Nichols explains that, 'Chesterton
does not regard childhood as a lost fairyland from
which adult life is merely an ever-accelerating descent
into reality. On the contrary, reality itself in its own
utterly non-necessary yet glorious being has the qualities that we normally ascribe to the realm of faëry.'[48]

## IV. The Fairytale as Truth

'The things I believed most then, the things I believe
most now, are the things called fairy tales.'[49] Chesterton believed that God speaks to us through everything,
but he had a particular delight in the way Divine Truth
is expressed through fairy tales. Via the fairytale,
man's moral dilemma is approached, not through the
complexities of philosophical discourse, but through
the simple imaginings and delights beholden within a
fairy tale. In administering to society's illnesses, Chesterton asserts that all things have value and point to
the simplicity and wisdom inherent in fairy tales:

> It is a great mistake to imagine that fairy tales
> are either immoral or unmoral. They do not
> tally with the trivialities of every particular
> moral code, but in this respect they resemble all
> works of art…In them we see the great lines of
> elementary laws and ideals as we see them
> nowhere else. We learn first and foremost that
> all doors fly open to courage and to hope. We
> learn that the world is bound together in mys-
> terious bonds of trust and compact and previ-
> sion, and that even green dragons keep their
> promises. We learn that nothing is wasted in
> the mills of the world, that a jewel thrown into
> the sea, a kindness to a stricken bird, an idle
> word to a ragged wayfarer, have in them some

terrible value and are here bound up with the destiny of men. Nothing is more typical and recurrent in the ethics of fairy tale than the great idea that nothing can be lost... The world is ruled by a sublime parsimony; there is no such thing as a dustbin in the house of God.[50]

The 'terrible value' of which Chesterton speaks are moral values; the moral choices by which one becomes a co-creator of life. This is the great and terrible gift of free will and what lends profundity to our thoughts and actions. 'In the fairy tale, an incomprehensible happiness rests upon an incomprehensible condition. A box is opened and all evils fly out. A word is forgotten and cities perish. A lamp is lit and love flies away. An apple is eaten and the hope of God is gone.'[51] Chesterton warns that it is imperative to be aware in which direction the mind and imagination travel. One doesn't have to be a theologian or philosopher to understand the great complexities to which Chesterton points. Appreciation of the profundity rooted within a fairytale is all that is needed. Chesterton comments:

This is one very characteristic moral of fairy tales, the idea of the indestructibility of an essence or an act. Another fully as common and even more essential is the great idea which lies at the heart of the story of 'Beauty and the Beast' and a hundred kindred tales; the idea that by loving a thing we make it beautiful. The fairy tale warns us to be on our guard against the disguises of things and to regard every ugly and repellent exterior with a hopeful and divine suspicion.[52]

Chesterton reminds us of the power of love and that our very lives are the most dramatic stories ever told.

Chesterton approaches the entire world with what could almost be called a 'theology of fairyland.' He makes this clear by stating, 'I am concerned with a certain way of looking at life, which was created by the fairy tales, but has since been meekly ratified by the mere facts.'[53] In *Heretics*, he writes:

> It is inspiriting without doubt to whizz in a motor-car round the earth, to feel Arabia as a whirl of sand or China as a flash of rice-fields. But Arabia is not a whirl of sand and China is not a flash of rice-fields. They are ancient civilizations with strange virtues buried like treasures. If we wish to understand them it must not be as tourists or inquirers, it must be with the loyalty of children and the great patience of poets. To conquer these places is to lose them. The man standing in his own kitchen-garden, with fairyland opening at the gate, is the man with large ideas. His mind creates distance; the motor-car stupidly destroys it.[54]

With use of the imagination, Chesterton allows the greatest philosophical complexities and the deepest theological dogmas to simply be assumed. Chesterton sees God as the author of the 'fairy tale' we now live. He doesn't reduce our lives to a fairytale but raises it to one. In doing so, evil and sin are not denied, nor is goodness spun into something sentimental. Chesterton's proper use of the imagination allows him to see ever more deeply into the mystery of creation:

> The things I believed most then, the things I believe most now, are the things called fairy tales. They seem to me to be the entirely reasonable things. They are not fantasies: compared with them other things are fantastic. Compared with them religion and rationalism are both

abnormal, though religion is abnormally right
and rationalism abnormally wrong. Fairyland
is nothing but the sunny country of common
sense. It is not earth that judges heaven, but
heaven that judges earth; so for me at least it
was not earth that criticized elfland, but elfland
that criticized the earth. I knew the magic
beanstalk before I had tasted beans; I was sure
of the Man in the Moon before I was certain of
the moon. This was at one with all popular
tradition. Modern minor poets are naturalists,
and talk about the bush or the brook; but the
singers of the old epics and fables were super-
naturalists, and talked about the gods of brook
and bush. That is what the moderns mean when
they say that the ancients did not 'appreciate
Nature,' because they said that Nature was
divine. Old nurses do not tell children about the
grass, but about the fairies that dance on the
grass; and the old Greeks could not see the trees
for the dryads.[55]

The innate truths found in fairytales exist in relation-
ships of love, particularly found in the family. This is
why, as K. Dwarakanath states,

Chesterton felt absolutely at home with children, who, he felt, are saner than adults because
they always live in a fairyland of wonder and
gratitude, unlike the adults who were either
ungrateful to God or dead to the miracles and
wonders of life around them. He was a boy
among boys, a philosopher among philosophers and a writer among writers, and the boy,
the philosopher, and the writer were blended
in that mass of flesh and spirit which was
always in an uninterrupted state of the essential
excitement of life.[56]

Just as a child delights in the love of his family without full comprehension, so also must the philosopher and theologian delight in what they can never fully comprehend.

When we step into the family, by the act of being born, we do step into a world which is incalculable, into a world which has its own strange laws, into a world which could do without us, into a world we have not made. In other words, when we step into the family we step into a fairy-tale.[57]

It is not imperative for us to fully comprehend the universe in which we live. It is the very nature of wonder *not* to comprehend. In *Robert Browning*, Chesterton draws our attention to this fact:

> It is well sometimes to half understand a poem in the same manner that we half understand the world. One of the deepest and strangest of all human moods is the mood which will suddenly strike us perhaps in a garden at night, or deep in sloping meadows, the feeling that every flower and leaf has just uttered something stupendously direct and important, and that we have by a prodigy of imbecility not heard or understood it. There is a certain poetic value, and that a genuine one, in this sense of having missed the full meaning of things. There is beauty, not only in wisdom, but in this dazed and dramatic ignorance.[58]

Within fairy tales, there is also a lesson to be learned about the mind's greatest enemy—fear.

But all these massive fragments of primitive morality are secondary to the great moral spirit which is the very heart of the fairy tales. That spirit is the principal appearing and reappearing in a thousand folklore stories, that nothing can do a man harm unless he fears it. At no time in the history of civilization, perhaps, has

there been so much need to recall the ethics of the
ancient warfare of Jack against the Giant, of the small
against the gigantic. Those who in our day express a
peculiar sympathy with the weak in their struggle
against the strong are often accused of indulging a
hypersensitive humanitarianism unknown to the
robuster ages of the world. The thing is a delusion. The
sympathy for the weak against the strong speaks out
of the oldest twilight; it is the very backbone of the
most savage stories with which we have to deal in
anthropology. For the fairy tale is the only history of
man himself, at once the weakest and the strongest of
the creatures.[59]

Chesterton, unlike Nietzsche's brand of nihilism,
sees compassion not as our greatest weakness, but as
our greatest strength. Part of that strength is being able
to see the world as God created it. Fairytales, Chesterton argues, introduce us to transcendental realities:

> Thinkers of [a certain] school have a tendency
> to believe that the concrete is the symbol of the
> abstract. The truth, the truth at the root of all
> mysticism, is quite the other way. The abstract
> is the symbol of the concrete. This may possibly
> seem at first sight a paradox; but it is a purely
> transcendental truth. We see a green tree. It is
> the green tree that we cannot understand; it is
> the green tree which we fear; it is the green tree
> which we worship. Then, because there are so
> many green trees, so many man, so many
> elephants, so many butterflies, so many daisies,
> so many animalculae, we coin a general term
> 'Life'. And then the mysticism comes and says
> that a green tree symbolized life. It is not so. Life
> symbolizes a green tree. Just in so far as we get
> into the abstract, we get away from the reality,

we get away from the mystery, we get away
from the tree. And this is the reason that so
many transcendental discourses are merely
blank and tedious to us, because they have to
do with Truth and Beauty and the Destiny of
the Soul and all the great faint, jaded symbols
of reality. And this is why poetry is so interesting to us, because it has to do with skies, with
woods, with battles, with temples, with women
and with wine, with the ultimate miracles
which no philosopher could create. The difference between the concrete and the abstract is
the difference between the country and the
town. God made the concrete, but man made
the abstract. A truthful man is a miracle, but the
truth is a commonplace.[60]

We needn't look far for the miraculous in life as we are
immersed in it. We are surrounded by profundity
beyond comprehension and Chesterton invites us to
see it, he invites us to discover with wonder the
staggering significance of our existence:

It is evident that, though all things are divine,
all things are limited. And among other divine
things, man himself is limited. He has not the
memory nor the imagination nor the vigilance
nor the sheer physical health to realize the
Godhead in every atom or object that passes
under his hands. A person who never neglected
any object: a man who burst into religious tears
as he fastened a divine collar with an inspired
collar-stud, and continued thus with everything
he looked at, would go mad in five minutes; he
would see God and die. The only things which
man, a limited animal, can do in this matter, are
two; first, he can believe (as an absolute thing
of faith) that there is this divinity in things,

whether he sees it or not; second, he can leave himself reasonable open to those sudden revelations whereby one or two of these things—a cloud, a man's face, a noise in the dark—may for some reason no one has ever been able to offer, capriciously reveal its divinity ...

I believe that every object is divine in a very definite and thorough sense. I believe, that is to say, that there is a great pleasure of spiritual reality behind things as they seem, and of this it affords of countless human affairs. And I believe that the supreme instance and the supreme demonstration of it is this; that if a man, dismissing the Cosmos and all such trifles, looks steadily and with some special and passionate adoration at some one thing, that thing suddenly speaks to him. Divinity lurks not in the All but in everything; and that, if it be true, is the explanation of a load of human chronicles, of a cataract of human testimony of all the religions, and all the wild tales of the world.... Providence desires its gifts received intensely and with humility and it is possible to look at one of them steadily and confidently until, with a great cry, it gives up its god.[61]

Chesterton looks to the cause of all things and traces everything back to the first cause: God. This is why he is able to perceive everything as miraculous; everything as possessing divine attributes. He moves, as it were, through a world of wonder and the miraculous. He sees mysticism in the simplest of things, everything speaks of mysticism because it is from God. Chesterton invites us, not to explain away or comprehend the universe we find ourselves in, but to dive into the wonderful created world of God. And, to do that, we need the trust of a child and the enthusiasm and humility of a child. Our very doubts must be turned into faith. To see goodness and know it has a source, to see beauty and ponder its origins, to encounter truth and know it to be your friend. This is what humility asks and what Chesterton reminds us of. In abandoning fears, doubts and presumptions, we become bold, certain, and assured. We become authentic supermen. When we allow ourselves to be loved by love all else is secondary. It is the only thing that matters. Chesterton points repeatedly, to what is of most interest to us, and to what is of most interest to God — our lives:

> People wonder why the novel is the most popular form of literature; people wonder why it is read more than books of science or books of metaphysics. The reason is very simple; it is merely that the novel is more true than they are. Life may sometimes legitimately appear as a book of science. Life may sometimes appear, and with a much greater legitimacy, as a book of metaphysics. But life is always a novel. Our existence may cease to be a song; it may cease even to be a beautiful lament. Our existence may not be an intelligible justice, or even a recognizable wrong. But our existence is still a story. In the fiery alphabet of every sunset is written, 'to be continued in our next.' If we have sufficient intellect, we can finish a philosophical and exact deduction, and be certain that we are finishing it right. With the adequate brain power we could finish any scientific discovery, and be certain that we are finishing it right. But not with the most gigantic intellect could we finish the simplest or silliest story, and be certain that we were finishing it right. That is because a story has behind it, not merely intel-

lect which is partly mechanical, but will, which is in its essence divine.[62]

Chesterton continually points to eternal truths found, not only in fairy tales, but in the depths of our human nature. Eternal truth speaks to the human soul in whatever form presented. We can recognizes these truths as real should they be found in religion, philosophy or politics. There is a motivation behind all that we human beings pursue, and that motivation is Truth. A motif that runs throughout much of Chesterton's writings is a type of full circle journey. A far-reaching search for truth that ends at home. He admits, 'I did try to found a little heresy of my own; and when I had put the last touches to it, I discovered that it was orthodoxy.'[63] This search for truth takes many forms and is part of our spiritual journey:

> It is not enough for a religion to include everything. It must include everything and something over. That is, it must include everything and include something as well. It must answer that deep and mysterious human demand for something as distinct from the demand for everything, even if the nature of that demand be too deep to be easily defined in logic. It will never cease to be described in poetry. We might almost say that all poetry is a description of it. Even when you have only natural religion, you will still have supernatural poetry. And it will be poetic because it is particular, not because it is general. The new priest may proclaim, 'The sea is God, the land is God and the sky is God; but yet there are not three Gods, but one God'. But even if the old priest is silenced the old poet will answer, 'God is in a cave; God is in a stable; God is disguised and hidden. I alone know

where he is; he is herding the cattle of Admetus, he is pouring out the wine of Cana.' The new republic may make the philosophical declaration, 'We hold these truths to be self-evident, that our trees are evolved equal and endowed with the dignity of creative evolution.' But if in the silence that follows we overhear the poor nurse or the peasant mother telling fairy tales to the children, she will always be saying, 'And in the seventh garden beyond the seventh gate was the tree with the golden apples'; or 'They sailed and sailed until they came to an island, and on the island was a meadow, and in the meadow the tree of life.'

In a word, *why* are all mysteries concerned with the notion of finding a particular thing in a particular place? If we are to find the real meaning of every element in mythology, what is the real meaning of *that* element in it? I can see only one possible answer that satisfies the new more serious and sympathetic study of religion, even among skeptics, and that is that there really is something to which all these fancies are what forgeries are to a signature; that if the soul could be satisfied with the truth, it would find it a tale as particular, as positive and as personal; that the light which we follow first as a wide white star actually narrows as we draw near to it, till we find that the trailing meteor is something like a light in a window or a candle in a room.[64]

Chesterton assists us in our struggles between fallen nature and divine allurements. In a very real way, he connects us to the love of God. If God is love then anything that is not love is not God. Our pride, both intellectual and imaginative, can construct, elaborate, and explore never-ending obstacles to the truth of God's love. Chesterton, with great simplicity, kindness, and compassion, reminds us that we are not only loved by God but loved and cherished in a particular way. Chesterton, by perceiving all things anew, challenges us to realize and to remember with hope that we are never alone on our pilgrimage.

Nietzsche sees God as a rival. And this mistaken perception is not uncommon in human history and human thought. In Robert Barron's *A Theology of Transformation,* we read:

> [There is] a tendency to place ourselves at the center of the universe, to render ourselves unconditioned and absolute. This false move of the spirit, in its turn, resulted in the objectification of all things and people around us: the god-ego threatened by rivals on all sides. And the greatest rival of all became God, that supreme being who must, at all costs, be either attacked or avoided, defeated or hidden from.[65]

The nihilistic approach is to attack and defeat God. It seeks to portray God as an unnecessary absurdity created by man. In his letter to G. K. Chesterton, Pope John Paul I remarks:

> They think that religion is a consolatory dream: it is supposed to have been invented by the oppressed, imagining a nonexistent world where they later will recover what is stolen from them today by their oppressors; it is supposed to have been organized, entirely for their own advantage, by those oppressors, to keep the oppressed still under their heel, and to lull in them that instinct of class which, without religion, would impel them to struggle.[66]

John Paul I finds an ally in Chesterton being fully
aware of Chesterton's genius in correcting distorted
views of the divine propagated by nihilism. In conclusion, the Pontiff ends his letter to G. K. Chesterton by
addressing those very attacks and attempts at defeat-
ing God:

> The one that many are fighting is not the true
> God, but the false idea of God that they have
> formed: a God who protects the rich, who only
> asks and demands, who is envious of our
> progress in well-being, who constantly observes
> our sins from above to enjoy the pleasure of
> punishing them!

> My dear Chesterton, you know as well as I, God
> is not like that, but is at once good and just;
> father also to prodigal sons; not wanting us
> poor and wretched, but great, free, creators of
> our own destiny. Our God is so far from being
> man's rival that He wanted man as a friend,
> calling him to share in His own divine nature
> and in His own eternal happiness. And it is not
> true that He makes excessive demands on us;
> on the contrary, He is satisfied with little,
> because He knows very well that we do not
> have much.

> Dear Chesterton, I am convinced, as you are:
> this God will become more and more known
> and loved, by everyone, including those who
> reject Him today, not because they are wicked
> (they may be better than either of us), but
> because they look at Him from a mistaken point
> of view! Do they continue not to believe in Him?
> Then He answers: I believe in you![67]

# Notes

1 Michael Ffinch, *G. K. Chesterton* (San Francisco: Harper & Row, 1986), 37.

2 G. K. Chesterton, *The Autobiography of G. K. Chesterton.* (New York: Sheed and Ward, 1936), 76-89.

3 Kevin C. Belmonte, *Defiant Joy: The Remarkable Life & Impact of G. K. Chesterton* (Nashville: Thomas Nelson, 2011), 21.

4 William Oddie, *Chesterton and the Romance of Orthodoxy: The Making of G. K.C.* 1874-1908 (New York:Oxford University Press, 2009),103.

5 George P. Landow is a professor of English and Art History at Brown University.

6 George P. Landow, 'Aesthetes and Decadents of the 1890s', *The Victorian Web: An Overview,* http://www.victorianweb.org/victorian/decadence/decadence.html, (accessed 12 December, 2012).

7 *Ibid.*

8 *Ibid.*

9 *The Autobiography of G. K. Chesterton,* 86.

10 *Ibid.,* 267.

11 K. Dwarakanath, *G. K. Chesterton: A Critical Study* (New Delhi: Classical Pub., 1986), 161.

12 Viktor E. Frankl, *Man's Search for Meaning: An Introduction to Logotherapy* (New York: Simon & Schuster, 1984), 133.

13 G. K. Chesterton, *Saint Thomas Aquinas* (New York: Sheed & Ward, 1933), 228.

14 Dorothy L. Sayers, *The Mind of the Maker* (London: Continuum, 2004), 116.

15 G. K. Chesterton, *The Man Who Was Orthodox: A Selection from the Uncollected Works of G. K. Chesterton,* ed. A. L. Maycock (London: Dennis Dobson, 1963), 170.

16 *The Autobiography of G. K. Chesterton,* 90.

17 G. K. Chesterton, *Orthodoxy* (New York: Dodd, Mead and Company, 1959), 56.

18 Henry T. Edmondson, *Return to Good and Evil: Flannery O'Connor's Response to Nihilism* (Lanham: Lexington Books, 2002), 20.

19 G. K. Chesterton, *George Bernard Shaw* (New York: John Lane, 1909), 198.

20   *Ibid.*, 199.

21   *Orthodoxy*, 22.

22   *George Bernard Shaw*, 199.

23   John R. Betz, 'Beyond The Sublime: The Aesthetics Of The Analogy Of Being (Part One)', *Modern Theology* 21, no. 3 (June 24, 2005)

24   G. K. Chesterton, *Heretics*, (New York: John Lane Company, 1905), 87.

25   Peter Kreeft, 'The Pillars of Unbelief', *National Catholic Register*, January 1988, 'Nietzsche', http://www.ncregister.com/.

26   Quentin Lauer, *G. K. Chesterton: Philosopher Without Portfolio* (New York: Fordham University Press, 1988), 74.

27   *Orthodoxy*, 65-76.

28   G. K. Chesterton, *Twelve Types* (London: A.L. Humphreys, 1906), 183.

29   Mark Armitage, 'The Riddles of God and the Solutions of Man: Chesterton's Metaphysics of Wonder', *The Chesterton Review: The Journal of the GK Chesterton Society* 27 (2001): 457-69.

30   *Saint Thomas Aquinas*, 207-10.

31   *The Autobiography of G. K. Chesterton*, 89.

32   Herbert Marshall McLuhan, cited in Hugh Kenner, *Paradox in Chesterton* (New York: Sheed & Ward, 1947), xii.

33   *Orthodoxy*, 96.

34   G. K. Chesterton, *St. Francis of Assisi* (New York: Image Books/Doubleday, 2001), 68.

35   *The Man Who Was Orthodox*, 170

36   G. K. Chesterton, cited in Maise Ward, *Gilbert Keith Chesterton* (New York: Sheed and Ward, 1943), 108-9.

37   *Saint Thomas Aquinas*, 6.

38   Dale Ahlquist, 'Who Is This Guy and Why Haven't I Heard of Him?', *The American Chesterton Society*, http://www.chesterton.org/wordpress/?page_id=40, (accessed 14 July, 2010).

39   G. K. Chesterton, *The Common Man* (London: Sheed and Ward, 1950), 12.

40   *Orthodoxy*, 207.

41   *G. K. Chesterton, Theologian*, 107.

42   G. K. Chesterton, *The Ballad of the White Horse* (New York: John Lane Company, 1916), 14.

43   *G. K. Chesterton, Theologian*, 108.

44  *The Common Man*, 137.
45  *Orthodoxy*, 296.
46  Peter Kreeft and Ellen Haroutunian, 'A Baptism of Imagination', *Leadership University*, July 13, 2002, http://leaderu.com/.
47  C. S. Lewis, *Surprised by Joy: The Shape of My Early Life* (New York: Harcourt Brace, 1995), 185.
48  G. K. Chesterton, *Theologian*, 110.
49  *George Bernard Shaw*, 87.
50  *The Man Who Was Orthodox*, 175.
51  *Orthodoxy*, 100.
52  *The Man Who Was Orthodox*, 176
53  *Orthodoxy*, 89.
54  *Heretics*, 52.
55  *Orthodoxy*, 87.
56  G. K. *Chesterton: A Critical Study*, 3.
57  *Heretics*, 192
58  G. K. Chesterton, *Robert Browning*, (New York: Macmillan Company, 1911), 158.
59  *The Man Who Was Orthodox*, 176.
60  *Ibid.*, 179.
61  *Ibid.*, 177.
62  *Heretics*, 193.
63  *Orthodoxy*, 19.
64  *The Man Who Was Orthodox*, 178.
65  Robert E. Barron, *And Now I See: A Theology of Transformation* (New York: Crossroad Publishing, 1998), 92.
66  Pope John Paul I, *Illustrissimi: Letters from Pope John Paul I*, trans. William Weaver (Boston: Little, Brown, 1978), 16.
67  *Ibid.*, 17.

# 2

# CHESTERTON AS THEOLOGIAN

*Just as it is better to illuminate than merely to shine,
so to pass on what one has contemplated is better
than merely to contemplate.*

Saint Thomas Aquinas

 RITING ABOUT G. K. Chesterton as theologian, Bernard Lonergan made a remarkable observation. If Chesterton, he wrote, had been writing in the eleventh century instead of the twentieth, he would be ranked today as a theologian with the status of St. Anselm:

> Then being a theologian was simply a matter of a cast of mind that seizes the fitness and coherence of the faith, that penetrates to its inner order and harmony and unity. Such penetration was the soul of Chesterton ...

> Such grasp of fitness and coherence is the essential object of the theologian at all times. But there is a further point in throwing Chesterton back upon the background of the medieval scene. More than any other modern man he shared the fresh and fearless vitality of medieval inquisitiveness. His questions go to the roots of things. The answers he demands must be right on the nail. He combined a whole-hearted contempt for the irrelevant with an ability to appreciate enormously, one might say inordinately, what really was relevant.[1]

Very often Chesterton penetrates to the 'root of things' by his use of paradox. While never oblivious to the existence of evil, he always sought to capture the essence and wonder of creation in all its forms. The object of Chesterton's theology is defined by wonder.

## I. The Use of Paradox

Chesterton's writing style is most notable for its use of paradox. While there are many who greatly admire this technique, there are still others who are much less impressed. In defense of Chesterton, Hugh Kenner writes,

> What appears to be superficial playing is really an intense plumbing among the mysterious roots of being and language; but in a sort of exhausted relief that this profound but disturbing visionary need not be read profoundly, his critics have neglected the intensity and enjoyed only the play.[2]

Chesterton's thinking is deeply theological yet presented poetically. In *Orthodoxy*, Chesterton articulates his theological intentions: 'I wish to set forth my faith as particularly answering this double spiritual need, the need for that mixture of the familiar and the unfamiliar which Christendom has rightly named romance.'[3]

Paradox is traditionally defined as, 'a statement that seems contradictory, unbelievable, or absurd but that may be true in fact.'[4] Chesterton certainly utilizes this understanding while employing both linguistic and philosophical paradox in his exposition of the Christian vision. In *Orthodoxy* he examines some key paradoxes inherent within the tradition of Christianity:

> Paganism declared that virtue was in a balance; Christianity declared it was in a conflict: the collision of two passions apparently opposite.

Of course they were not really inconsistent; but there was such that it was hard to hold simultaneously ... Christianity thus held a thought on the dignity of man that could only be expressed in crowns rayed like the sun and fans of peacock plumage. Yet at the same time it could hold a thought about the abject smallness of man that could only be expressed in fasting and fantastic submission, in the gray ashes of St. Dominic and the white snows of St. Bernard ... Here, again, in short, Christianity got over the difficulty of combining furious opposites, by keeping them both, and keeping them both furious. The Church was positive on both points. One can hardly think too little of one's self. One can hardly think too much of one's soul.[5]

For Chesterton, paradox is an attempt to express the inexpressible. He uses it as a tool to approach the unapproachable; the ideas he is trying to express strain human language. He employs paradox so frequently because he often engages the great 'both/and' nature of Christianity. The Christian tradition cannot be reduced to a singularity or pigeon-holed into a tidy definition. Commenting about Chesterton on one occasion, Robert Barron remarks as follows on Christianity's innately paradoxical character:

On the one hand, Christianity—especially Catholicism—was criticized for being too worldly, too caught up in wealth, property, pomp, and ceremony. Where, for instance, was the spirit of the carpenter of Nazareth in the expensive theatrical display of the Vatican? On the other hand, Christianity was reviled for its excessive spiritualism, its indifference to the concrete concerns of the world, its tendency to pine after the 'things of heaven.' Similarly, some critics complained that Christianity, with its stress on sin, penitence, and punishment, was excessively pessimistic, while others held that, given its emphasis on the love of God, the intervention of the saints, and the promise of eternal life, it was ridiculously optimistic. Finally, certain enemies of the faith maintained, probably with Joan of Arc and the Crusades in mind, that Christianity was bloodthirsty and warlike, while others held, probably with Francis in mind, that it was too pacific and nonviolent. What puzzled Chesterton, of course, was not that the Church had its critics, but that its critics were so varied, so at odds with one another, so mutually exclusive. Whatever this Christianity was, he concluded, it must be something strangely shaped indeed to inspire such a wildly divergent army of enemies.[6]

Chesterton is quite often approaching realities beyond the scope of human comprehension and utilizes daring paradoxes to express his vision of Christianity. Andrè Maurois is aware of both the strengths and weaknesses of this approach:

Chesterton, with wonderful vigour and brilliance, has striven to reconcile intelligence with tradition. Against Shaw and Wells he is an indispensable counterpoise ...

He can be accused of sometimes falling victim to his own virtuosity. The physicist works out symmetrical formulas and finds in these the laws of the universe because God is a geometrist; similarly Chesterton, by setting paradox alongside paradox, builds up a picture of reality because reality is a totaling of paradoxes. But sometimes this juggling with formulas exhausts the reader, who is left with an uneasy feeling in his mind. He sees so clearly that Chesterton is brilliant that he no longer sees how profound Chesterton is. In the ballet of his words we do not always recognize the ordinary life which he would have us love ...

Without his paradoxes, without his jokes, without his rhetorical switchbacks, Chesterton might perhaps be a clearer philosopher. But he would not be Chesterton. It has often been supposed that he is not serious, because he is funny; actually he is funny because he is serious. Confident in his truth, he can afford to joke ... Certainty breeds serenity.[7]

In a similar vein Hugh Kenner remarks: 'Chesterton must be taken seriously because paradox must be taken seriously, both as a tool of expression and as an ingredient of reality.'[8] This can be seen in *Orthodoxy* where Chesterton takes the meaning of courage into the profoundest depths of Christianity:

Let us follow for a moment the clue of the martyr and the suicide; and take the case of courage. No quality has ever so much addled the brains and tangled the definitions of merely rational sages. Courage is almost a contradiction in terms. It means a strong desire to live taking the form of a readiness to die. 'He that will lose his life, the same shall save it' ... This paradox is the whole principle of courage; even of quite earthly or quite brutal courage ... A soldier surrounded by enemies, if he is to cut his way out, needs to combine a strong desire for living with a strange carelessness about dying. He must not merely cling to life, for then he will be a coward, and will not escape. He must seek his life in a spirit of furious indifference to it; he must desire life like water and yet drink death like wine. No philosopher, I fancy, has ever expressed this romantic riddle with adequate lucidity, and I certainly have not done so. But Christianity has done more: it has marked the limits of it in the awful graves of the suicide and the hero, showing the distance between him who dies for the sake of living and him who dies for the sake of dying ... the Christian courage, which is a disdain of death; not the Chinese courage, which is a disdain of life.[9]

Chesterton seeks to regain the vision necessary to perceive the Eden that is all around us. Through his use of analogy and paradox he explains that, 'The mind and eyes of the average man in this world is as lost as Eden and as sunk as Atlantis.'[10] Yes, we are indeed blind to the beauty and truth that radiates towards us and, given our tendency towards pride, we must be vigilant. But Chesterton warns of another tendency that is far worse. He cautions:

There runs a strange law through the length of human history—that men are continually tending to undervalue their environment, to undervalue their happiness, to undervalue themselves. The great sin of mankind, the sin typified by the fall of Adam, is the tendency, not towards pride, but towards this weird and horrible humility.[11]

We think little of ourselves. We hardly dare to think how truly remarkable is the universe which surrounds us. Chesterton writes: 'Most probably we are in Eden still. It is only our eyes that have changed.'[12]

Although he uses paradox, for Chesterton it is not merely a literary device. Paradox for him was the only conceivable way for the human mind to approach truths that are inconceivable. Christianity, for Chesterton, was the ultimate paradox. He never presumes to know a truth in its entirety, but he does, through his use of paradox, catch glimpses of it. His mind races from one truth to the next and, as readers, we are invited to follow—fast on his heels—the bright traces of paradox.

One celebrated modern author who allowed himself to be greatly influenced by Chesterton was J. R. R. Tolkien. In a moving letter sent to his son, Tolkien points to the paradox and passion lying at the heart of Christianity:

> Out of the darkness of my life, so much frustrated, I put before you the one great thing to love on earth: the Blessed Sacrament ... There you will find romance, glory, honour, fidelity, and the true way of all your loves on earth, and more than that: Death. By the divine paradox, that which ends life, and demands the surrender of all, and yet by the taste—or foretaste—of which alone can what you seek in your earthly relationships (love, faithfulness, joy) be maintained, or take on that complexion of reality, of eternal endurance, which every man's heart desires.[13]

Nihilism would reduce all of reality, including the world of human beings, to insignificance. In contrast, Christianity elevates and enlightens the human being far beyond his own capacity. And, standing at the very center of that enlightenment, is the greatest paradox of all—the Cross. What appears, at first, as a broken symbol of destruction and stupidity is, in fact, Chesterton explains, a beacon of 'mystery and health'. He contrasts the cruciform shape of the Cross with that of a perfectly round circle:

> For the circle is perfect and infinite in nature; but it is fixed forever in its size; it can never be larger

or smaller. But the cross, though it has at its heart
a collision and a contradiction, can extend its
four arms forever without altering its shape.
Because it has a paradox in its centre it can grow
without changing. The circle returns upon itself
and is bound. The cross opens its arms to the four
winds; it is a signpost for free travelers.[14]

## II. Chesterton of the Creator

On one occasion, Joseph Ratzinger remarked:

> G. K. Chesterton was often blessed with the gift
> of a striking turn of phrase. He certainly hit upon
> a decisive aspect of the work of St. Thomas
> Aquinas when he observed that, if the great doctor
> were to be given a name in the style of the Car-
> melite Order ('of the Child Jesus,' 'of the Mother
> of God,' etc.), he would have to be called Thomas
> a Creatore, 'Thomas of the Creator.' Creator and
> creation are the core of his theological thought.[15]

Almost the entire canon of Chesterton's writing centers
around the wonder of existence, the fact that there is
being instead of non-being. This is the reality which
confronts, confounds, and ultimately conquers Chesterton's intellect into submissive wonder. And, of course,
it was what saved him from despair as a young man,
and kept him afloat when he found himself almost
submerged by the dark and dangerous waters of nihilism.

Linked with Chesterton's awareness of a Creator as
the source of all things is his conviction regarding
'philosophical realism'. On this subject Richard Gill
writes:

> According to G. K. Chesterton, one of the main
> delusions to which we can succumb is the belief
> that the outside world is created by the self. In

combating this illusion, Chesterton defends philosophical realism—the belief that the objects of thought have a real existence independent of the thoughts of the inquirer. Idealist thinkers, in this account, fail to do justice to the otherness of existence, for its origin is not recognized as situated outside the self. In contrast to the thought of the idealists, and against materialist reductionists who would deny that there is any Creator to whom we can express our gratitude, Chesterton ultimately came to understand his realist perspective in relation to the philosophy of St. Thomas Aquinas. Philosophically a realist, Chesterton asserted that his politics were those of a radical idealist, and he maintained that the relativism which stemmed from anti-realism would be useless for the attainment of a genuinely radical social agenda.

By coming to recognize existence as a gift which elicits the response of gratitude, Chesterton extracted himself from a youthful solipsism and found himself to be deeply at odds with what he perceived to be the dominant theories of the intellectual establishment. Chesterton found the sciences promoting a reductionist materialism and the arts engulfed by an atmosphere of idealism with both camps positively hostile to the Judeo-Christian heritage which understood existence as a miraculous gift of God's Creation. Materialists understood nature as mere matter in motion, subject to its own inexorable laws. They denied the supernatural dimension of reality—the existence of a Creator to whom we could express our gratitude. Philosophical idealism, by contrast, through which an individual came to perceive the world as the creation of

their own minds, led to the denial of any natural
reality that could be the object of wonder.[16]

Within creation Chesterton finds the solace of certitude. No matter how dark and dismal the world may
become, the fact remains that it still exists. It exists
because it has been created and Chesterton finds
himself alive as a man within Creation. Nowhere can
he look and not see it. For Chesterton, it is not simply
a matter of appreciation: creation is always telling a
story, a story full of profundities beyond human
comprehension. In The Resurrection of Rome, Chesterton travels through the Eternal City and examines
it through his lens of wonder. Commenting on the
amazing display of statuary and painting etc., and
certain critical reactions to it, Chesterton remarks:

> They speak more truly than they know who say
> that the sign and scandal of the Catholic Church
> is the Graven Image. The Church forbids us to
> worship it save as a symbol; but as a symbol it
> is most solidly symbolic. For it stands for this
> strange mania of Certitude, without which
> Rome will remain a riddle; it stands for the
> intolerant and intolerable notion that something
> is really true; true in every aspect and from
> every angle; true from the four quarters of the
> sky; true by the three dimensions of the Trinity.
> We turn from it and it does not vanish; we
> analyze it and it does not dissolve; at last, after
> long and laborious experiments in skepticism,
> we are forced to believe our eyes.[17]

Concerning the writings of G. K. Chesterton, W. H.
Auden observes: 'Both in his prose and in his verse, he
sees, as few writers have, the world about him as full
of sacramental signs or symbols.'[18] The Churches of

Rome have at times been criticized for being overly ornate. In the opinion of some people all the marble and mosaics, all the sculpture and the paintings, are simply too much. They bombard and offend the senses. But, for Chesterton, these Renaissance and Baroque works of art are not overly ostentatious. They are a 'blare of trumpets',[19] he writes, heralding 'the special sort of energy we have seen everywhere in this history; the energy of the resurrection.'[20] Chesterton is able to see what might appear grandiose with the innocent eyes of a child. Of the many sights of Rome he remarks: 'They remind me of the bold scenery of a pantomime or a toy-theatre, and even St. Peter's Dome sometimes looks like Aladdin's Palace.'[21]

Concerning Chesterton's approach to Creation, one commentator observes: 'One could say that at the root his goodness was his extraordinarily acute awareness of the need to be grateful for the abundant gifts that make up both mystery and the exhilarating experience of life, of existence.'[22] It is exactly this openness to the miracle of life and existence that allowed Chesterton to live in a constant state of wonder. He declares as much in his Autobiography:

> I had in childhood, and have partly preserved out of childhood, a certain romance of receptiveness, which has not been killed by sin or even by sorrow; for though I have not had great troubles, I have had many. A man does not grow old without being bothered; but I have grown old without being bored. Existence is still a strange thing to me and as a stranger I give it welcome.[23]

The simple fact of existence continually haunts and surprises Chesterton. He speaks of it with an almost

unparalleled eloquence in the following passage from
one of his books:

> There is at the back of all our lives an abyss of
> light, more blinding and unfathomable than any
> abyss of darkness; and it is the abyss of actual-
> ity, of existence, of the fact that things truly are,
> and that we ourselves are and incredibly and
> sometimes real. It is the fundamental fact of
> being, as against not being; it is unthinkable, yet
> we cannot unthink it, though we may some-
> times be unthinking about it; unthinking and
> especially unthanking. For he who realized this
> reality knows that it does outweigh, literally to
> infinity, all lesser regrets or arguments for
> negation, and that under all our grumblings
> there is a subconscious substance of gratitude.[24]

The shock of existence is, for Chesterton, the starting
point for opening up his mind to the Source behind
Creation, and to the revelation of that Source in Christ
Jesus. His lens of wonder shines brightest when held
to the light of divine revelation. Chesterton never
ceases to be amazed by the marvel and meaning of the
redemption won for us by Christ, by the fact that now
in truth our innocence has been restored. The memo-
ries of his childhood, which he so dearly cherished, are
no longer pangs of nostalgia but have been saved and
made new again. Remarking on his journey through
dogmas and doctrines, Chesterton concludes:

> One can find no meanings in a jungle of skepti-
> cism; but the man will find more and more
> meanings who walks through a forest of doc-
> trine and design. Here everything has a story
> tied to its tail, like the tools or pictures in my
> father's house; for it is my father's house I end
> where I began—at the right end. I have entered

at least the gate of all good philosophy. I have
come into my own second childhood.[25]

Perceiving the Divine in all things was not an escapist
form of spirituality for Chesterton. As an author, he
was reacting to the cultural crisis of his time. He
wanted to uphold and showcase the everlasting truths
that were being discarded by the intelligentsia of his
day. In doing so, he reacted with determined force to
swing the pendulum far the other way. This has led
some of his detractors to accuse Chesterton of being
unrealistically optimistic with an absurd childlike view
of reality. Is there any basis in reality for this criticism?
In his enthusiasm for all that is good in the world, does
he in fact ignore the horrendous fact of evil?

## III. What Evil May Come

Reviewing *The Defendant*, C. F. G. Masterman considers
Chesterton's approach to reality to be lacking in depth
and honesty. 'Mr. Chesterton is convinced that the Devil
is dead. A children's epileptic hospital, a City diner, a
suburban at home, a South African charnel camp, or
any other examples of cosmic ruin failed to shake this
blasphemous optimism.'[26] Masterman was not alone in
finding fault with Chesterton's sanguinity. The criticisms by Henry Murray on Chesterton are comparable:

> The real paradox about Mr. Chesterton—or
> rather, one of the many real paradoxes he illus-
> trates—is that, with a tender and overflowing
> affection for all sentient things, he seems almost
> completely ignorant of the existence of sorrow
> and suffering. And this strange ignorance or
> carelessness of the facts of everyday life marks
> the limit of his powers. He has amused and
> tickled thousands ... but I cannot imagine that

he has ever given one solitary individual a moist
eye or a lump in the throat. Pathos and tragedy
are notes, or rather entire octaves, lacking from
his keyboard. His boisterous optimism will not
admit that there's anything to sorrow over in this
best of all possible worlds.[27]

I would suggest that to accuse Chesterton of complete
ignorance of 'sorrow and suffering' is to completely
miss the point of Chesterton's rhetoric. The Edwardian
cultural crisis is exemplified through Murray's reaction
to Chesterton and certainly 'marks the limits' of its own
powers by referring to Chesterton's 'optimism'. At the
heart of Murray's criticisms is the notion that sorrow
and suffering should be the principal concern of a
writer. It is not difficult to understand why evil would
be a primary focus for a writer but the prominence
Murray gives to it is important in understanding Chesterton. Considering the way in which time had reduced
Chesterton's standing as a writer by 1944, Graham
Greene deduced it was because the two world wars had
brought suffering to the forefront of the nation's mind:

> We are already proving our eccentricity in the
> case of Chesterton: a generation that appreciates
> Joyce finds for some reason Chesterton's
> equally fanatical play on words exhausting.
> Perhaps it is that he is still suspected of levity,
> and the generation now reaching middle-age
> has been a peculiarly serious one.[28]

The question proposed by Evelyn Waugh concurs with
this assessment of Chesterton:

> Could Chesterton have written like that today,
> if he had lived to see the Common Man in arms,
> drab, gray and brown, the Storm Troopers and
> the Partisans, standard-bearers of the great

popular movements of the century; had he lived
to read in the evidence of the War Trials the
sickening accumulation of brutality inflicted
and condoned by common men?[29]

Interesting as Waugh's inquiry is, the accusations
leveled against Chesterton by his critics show that the
problem of evil was intensely felt long before the
Second World War. One could argue that there was a
certain fascination with evil among many of Chesterton's contemporaries. Contrary to the presumption
that Chesterton's 'optimism' signifies an inability to
engage the reality of evil, it correctly signifies a proper
response to evil. As Chesterton himself explains:
'Perhaps, when I eventually emerged as a sort of
theorist, and was described as an Optimist, was
because I was one of the few people in the world of
diabolism who really believed in devils.'[30] Chesterton,
in his essay 'On Original Sin', clearly states the need
for evil to be taken seriously:

> Men who wish to get down to fundamentals
> perceive that there is a fundamental problem of
> evil. Men content to be more superficial are also
> content with a superficial fuss and bustle of
> improvement. The man in the mere routine of
> modern life is content to say that a modern
> gallows is a relatively human instrument or that
> a modern cat-o'-nine-tails is milder than ancient
> Roman *flagellum*. But the original thinker will
> ask why any scourge or gibbet was ever needed,
> or ever even alleged to be needed? And that
> brings the original thinker back to original sin.[31]

Chesterton is an original thinker, not because his
thoughts are entirely original, but because he does not
allow the fog of modernity to interfere with his per-

ception of reality and the ugly truths to be found submerged within the soul of mankind. Chesterton's critics fail to recognize his theological intuition and therefore miss, entirely, a very real and vibrant Christocentric perspective. Chesterton acknowledges evil and understands it deeply on a theological level; not only with regard to Original Sin and the demonic but in relation to Christ:

> I purposely insist first on this optimistic, I might almost say this pantheistic or even this pagan aspect of the Christian Gospels. For it is only when we understand that Christ, considered merely as a prophet, can be and is a popular leader in the love of natural things, that we can feel that tremendous and tragic energy of his testimony to an ugly reality, the existence of unnatural things. Instead of taking a text as I have done, take a whole Gospel and read it steadily and honestly and straight through at a sitting, and you will certainly have one impression, whether of a myth or of a man. It is that the exorcist towers above the poet and even the prophet; that the story between Cana and Calvary is one long war with demons. He understood better than a hundred poets the beauty of the flowers of the battle-field; but he came out to battle. And if most of his words mean anything they do mean that there is at our very feet, like a chasm concealed among the flowers, an unfathomable evil ... it is here [at Sodom] that tradition has laid the tragedy of the mighty perversion of the imagination of man; the monstrous birth and death of abominable things. I say such things in no mood of spiritual pride; such things are hideous not because they are distant but because they are

near to us; in all our brains, certainly in mine,
were buried things as bad as any buried under
that bitter sea, and if He did not come to do
battle with them, even in the darkness of the
brain of man, I know not why He came.[32]

Chesterton knows evil well and is certainly not ignorant
of it. He chooses a proper response to it by focusing on
that which is greater. He concentrates his efforts on
something far more powerful and far more astounding
than evil could imagine: the great goodness of God.
Mark Knight provides some crucial historical context
regarding Chesterton's awareness of evil:

To understand Chesterton's treatment of evil it
is necessary to begin with his response to some
of the philosophical trends of the 1890s.
Looking back at the ideas he found so troubling
during his time at the Slade School of Art,
Chesterton identified a negative and nihilistic
philosophy as being at the heart of contemporary thought. To appreciate what this philosophy entailed, it is helpful to begin by noting
Nietzsche's rejection of absolutes—both ethical
and otherwise—and to relate this to the thought
of Wilde. Chesterton's critique of attempts to
blur the boundaries between good and evil is
central to his tale 'The Diabolist,' a tale that
invites certain comparisons with Wilde's *The
Picture of Dorian Gray*. With the aid of theology,
Chesterton sought to reconstruct a clear demar-
cation between good and evil, although he
acknowledged that individual persons could
not be described simply as one or the other. The
attempt to distinguish between good and evil
is apparent throughout the Father Brown stories, and the chapter turns to these tales in an
effort to articulate Chesterton's understanding

of the nature of evil. To avoid the dangers of
dualism (which grants evil ontological auton-
omy) and monism (which tends toward the
suggestion that evil is merely an illusion), the
Father Brown stories follow Augustine and
Aquinas in thinking of evil as privation.[33]

The great challenge in 'portraying evil as privation' in
a creative manner is keeping a story interesting, which
Chesterton does well. He never denies the existence of
evil, nor does he allow it to have its own power. This
can be seen in Knight's observations of Chesterton's
fictional work. Too often in the age of modernity evil
is not portrayed in an authentic way, evil is either
reduced as an alternative form of good or simply
denied as existing at all. The French poet Charles
Baudelaire famously wrote 'do not ever forget, when
you hear the progress of lights praised, that the love-
liest trick of the Devil is to persuade you that he does
not exist!'[34] This is a statement to which Chesterton
would happily have assented. As much as anyone
Chesterton has a keen awareness of the existence of
evil and knows its trappings and insidious workings
very well. His acknowledgment of evil, while certainly
being intellectual, stems primarily from his first-hand
personal experience with the diabolic.

Chesterton may have been accused of, 'blasphemous optimism,' but a sincere inquiry into his work
proves that the accusation is unfounded. It's not that
Chesterton denied evil or even chose to look away
from it, he was simply enthralled and far more inter-
ested in a greater form of existence: the existence of
good. Robert Barron correctly points out,

> It was Chesterton who remarked that the only
> problem more puzzling than the question of

evil is the question of good. What accounts, in
the end, for our confidence in the face of the
overwhelming warrant for despair? Why do we
keep breathing in and out; why do we go on
even when everything around us says,
"Stop"?'[35]

The answer to those questions is the existence of good,
which proves in the tradition of Aquinas and others,
to be far more powerful and influential than evil. To
correctly see evil as a privation is to correctly see the
world as it is and to correctly have hope in the existence of goodness.

Offering further defense to Chesterton's acknowledgment of evil is Gary Wills. Comparing *The Wild
Knight* to *The Diabolist*, Wills gives this account:

We can see, in the poem, turmoil giving birth
to insight. The insight is metaphysical, as was
the problem, and arises from the mind's
encounter with evil. Thus *The Wild Knight*
completely invalidates the assumption that
Chesterton's 'dark years' were simply a time of
physical and moral 'growing pains,' and it
invalidates the logical inference to be drawn
from such a reading of his history—drawn with
effect by Kenner and others—that Chesterton
was a person jolly and contented by nature,
who never had to struggle or know evil. Evil
precipitated, at a time of stress, the very metaphysical insight which Kenner praises in Chesterton. It is true that Chesterton felt evil as a
final puzzle and blank for the brain, as well as
a tugging at the will; but this only made its
negations more absolute and terrifying. An
almost suicidal mental rapidity made him turn
people and events into ideas, ideas which could
be annihilated with an argument. A metaphys-

ical insight rescued him at this stage, checking
the intellect's headlong course; but this could
not change the general tendency of his mind.
He still felt an idea like a blow and saw the
significance of real things with painful clarity.
This, and not the subhuman complacency often
attributed to him, is the reason Chesterton's
mind works rapidly into depth, probing and
rebounding and debating.[36]

Those who criticize Chesterton's optimism are failing
to see Chesterton's metaphysical perspectives as well
as his Thomistic approach to reality. In a world perme-
ated by nihilism, there are those who are incapable of
approaching reality this way. When confronted or
exposed to it, they mistake it for something other than
what it truly is. The true becomes false and the false
becomes true. This is the philosophical mistake lodged
in the heart of a nihilistic culture. When a culture is
blinded by a philosophy that promotes the will and
the ego, the experience of reality is diminished.

The perspective on pain and suffering and the
problem of evil is likewise diminished, or at least not
seen correctly, and this can result in tragic consequences. Chesterton once explained that, 'There is the
tragedy that is founded on the worthlessness of life; and
there is the deeper tragedy that is founded on the worth
of it. The one sort of sadness says that life is so short
that it can hardly matter; the other that life is so short
that it will matter forever.'[37] Once again, Chesterton's
use of paradox portrays a truth: our tragedy is to refuse
the full significance of our lives and deeds. For the fact
is that all our moral acts, all our moral decisions,
resonate throughout eternity. Chesterton, by celebrating
man's higher calling, does not deny evil, he simply
refuses to stare forever at the wreckage of human

failings. As a thinker, and a man of faith, he looks through and beyond our misery, and it is the quality of that looking which makes him not just a helpful commentator on matters of the day but a worthy theologian.

## Notes

1   Bernard Lonergan, S.J., 'Chesterton the Theologian', *The Chesterton Review*, Spring/Summer, 30, no. 1/2 (2004).
2   Hugh Kenner, *Paradox in Chesterton* (New York: Sheed & Ward, 1947), 4.
3   G. K. Chesterton, *Orthodoxy* (New York: Dodd, Mead and Company, 1959), 15.
4   Michael Agnes, ed., *Webster's New World College Dictionary*, 4th ed. (Cleveland: Wiley Publishing, 2007), s.v. 'Paradox'.
5   *Orthodoxy*, 170–174.
6   Robert Barron, *Bridging the Great Divide: Musings of a Post-liberal, Post-Conservative, Evangelical Catholic* (Lanham: Rowman & Littlefield Publishers, 2004), 5.
7   Andrè Maurois, cited in Joseph Pearce, *Wisdom and Innocence: A Life of G. K. Chesterton* (San Francisco: Ignatius Press, 1996), 463.
8   Kenner, *Paradox in Chesterton*, 5.
9   *Orthodoxy*, 170.
10  G. K. Chesterton, *The Defendant* (New York: Dodd, Mead and Company, 1902), 3.
11  *Ibid.*
12  *Ibid.*
13  J. R. R.Tolkien, cited in Stratford Caldecott, *Secret Fire: The Spiritual Vision of J.R. Tolkien* (London: Darton Longman & Todd, 2003), 64.
14  *Orthodoxy*, 50.
15  Joseph Ratzinger, *In the Beginning: A Catholic Understanding of the Story of Creation and the Fall* (Grand Rapids: W.B. Eerdmans Publishing Company, 1995), 79.
16  Richard Gill, 'Chesterton's Realism,' *Renascence: Essays on Values in Literature* 57, no. 3 (2005), 1.
17  G. K. Chesterton, *The Resurrection of Rome,* (New York: Dodd, Mead &, 1930), 75.

18    W. H. Auden, cited in John Sullivan, ed., *G. K. Chesterton. A Centenary Appraisal* (London: Harper & Row Publishers, 1974), 76.

19    G. K. Chesterton, *The Resurrection of Rome,* (New York: Dodd, Mead &, 1930), 158.

20    *Ibid.*

21    *Ibid.,* 157.

22    Quentin Lauer, *G. K. Chesterton: Philosopher Without Portfolio,* 16.

23    G. K. Chesterton, *The Autobiography of G. K. Chesterton.* (New York: Sheed and Ward, 1936), 352.

24    G. K. Chesterton, *Chaucer,* (New York: Greenwood Press, 1969), 32.

25    *Orthodoxy,* 293.

26    C. F. G. Masterman, cited in D. J. Conlon, *G. K. Chesterton: The Critical Judgments* (Antwerp: Universitaire Faculteiten Sint-Ignatius, 1976), 42.

27    Henry Murray, cited in Conlon, *G. K. Chesterton: The Critical Judgments* 237.

28    Graham Greene, cited in Denis Joseph Conlon, ed., *G. K. Chesterton a Half Century of Views* (Oxford: Oxford University Press, 1987), 59.

29    Evelyn Waugh, cited in Conlon, *A Half Century of Views,* 74.

30    *The Autobiography of G. K. Chesterton,* 89.

31    G. K. Chesterton, 'On Original Sin' (1930), *In Defense of Sanity: The Best Essays of G. K. Chesterton,* ed., Dale Ahlquist (San Francisco, Ignatius Press 2011) p.193.

32    G. K. Chesterton, *The New Jerusalem* (New York: George H. Doran Company, 1921), 192–195.

33    Knight, *Chesterton and Evil,* 29.

34    Charles Baudelaire, cited in Maximilian J. Rudwin, ed., *Devil Stories; an Anthology,* trans. Arthur Symons (New York: A.A. Knopf, 1921), 164.

35    Robert E. Barron, *And Now I See--: A Theology of Transformation* (New York: Crossroad Publishing, 1998), 22.

36    Garry Wills, *Chesterton, Man and Mask.* (New York: Sheed & Ward, 1961), 31.

37    G. K. Chesterton, 'The Character of King Edward' (4 June 1910), *The Illustrated London News 1908–10,* vol. 28 of *The Collected Works of G. K. Chesterton* (San Francisco: Ignatius Press, 1987), 540.

# 3

# THE CALL TO WONDER

*Because philosophy arises from awe, a philosopher is bound in his way to be a lover of myths and poetic fables. Poets and philosophers are alike in being big with wonder.*

St Thomas Aquinas

N THE WORLD of modernity, where scientific certitude is heralded as supreme knowledge, there is something that has been neglected. The imagination has become deadened to the truth and profundity of existence. It no longer stands in awe of creation but waits for a dull explanation. Chesterton beckons one to move beyond the confines of mere logic and knowledge to recapture the glorious 'light of wonder' that once held and dazzled the human imagination. Chesterton calls for a contemplative outlook which can be rightly termed a call to wonder.

## I. Reason beyond Logic

Chesterton's contemplative outlook can be seen in *The Everlasting Man* where he attempts to illuminate mankind's spiritual pilgrimage. The work was a direct rebuttal of H. G. Wells' *Outline of History* which denied Creationism as well as the divinity of Christ. Chesterton had a clear Christocentric lens by which he viewed reality. Anything that may be called a theology of wonder, pertaining to Chesterton, can always be seen through this lens. With regard to the event of the resurrection, for example, he wrote:

> On the third day the friends of Christ coming at daybreak to the place found the grave empty and the stone rolled away. In varying ways they realized the new wonder; but even they hardly realized that the world had died in the night. What they were looking at was the first day of a new creation, with a new heaven and a new earth; and in a semblance of the gardener God walked again in the garden, in the cool not of the evening but the dawn.[1]

Chesterton's perception of reality is radically different from that of the intellectual elitists of his day, from the materialists, for example, who were unable to see reality beyond matter, and from the solipsists, who were unable to see it beyond their own minds. As he states in *Orthodoxy*:

> The man who cannot believe his senses [the solipsist] and the man who cannot believe anything else [the materialist] are both insane, but their insanity is proved not by any error in their argument, but by the manifest mistake of their whole lives. They have both locked themselves up in two boxes, painted inside with the sun and stars; they are both unable to get out, the one into the health and happiness of heaven, the other even into the health and happiness of the earth.[2]

In *The Thing; Why I Am a Catholic*, Chesterton develops this criticism of the intellectual ethos of his day. He writes:

> Freethinkers are occasionally thoughtful, though never free. In the modern world of the West, at any rate, they seem always to be tied to the

treadmill of a materialist and monist cosmos.
The universal skeptic, in Asia or in Antiquity,
has probably been a bolder thinker, though very
probably a more unhappy man. But what we
have to deal with as skepticism is not skepticism;
but a fixed faith in monism. He is forbidden, for
instance, in the only intelligible modern sense,
to believe in a miracle.[3]

Chesterton was not opposed, in any way, to logical
explanations. He was simply aware of the risks of
applying strict logic to the deepest truths and mysteries of human life. Chesterton believed in miracles. And
since he knew God to be the first cause of all things,
all things to him were miraculous. He writes:

Let it be noted that this is not, as is always
loosely imagined, a reaction against material
science; or a regret for mechanical invention; or
a depreciation for telephones or telescopes or
anything else. It is exactly the other way. I am
not depreciating telephones; I am complaining
that they are not appreciated. I am not attacking
inventions; I am attacking indifference to inventions. I only remark that it is the same people
who brag about them who are really indifferent
to them. I am not objecting to the statement that
the science of the modern world is wonderful;
I am only objecting to the modern world
because it does not wonder at it.[4]

What Chesterton viewed as really tragic was for a
human being not to see the world, and all that is in it,
as miraculous. He knew all too well how easily people
are led by new and popular trends of thought,
beguiled by movements or philosophies which often
end up not by liberating their followers but by impris-
oning them. He remarked: 'A new philosophy gener-

ally means in practice the praise of some old vice.'[5]
Chesterton accepts the surprise of existence uncondi-
tionally, without endeavoring, as did some of his
contemporaries, to fit it into some fabricated logical
construct. Imprison people in a formulaic world, he
tells us, and they will go mad.

> Mysticism keeps men sane. As long as you have
> mystery you have health; when you destroy
> mystery you create morbidity. The ordinary
> man has always been sane because the ordinary
> man has always been a mystic. He has permit-
> ted the twilight. He has always had one foot in
> earth and the other in fairyland. He has always
> left himself free to doubt his gods; but (unlike
> the agnostic of to-day) free also to believe in
> them. He has always cared more for truth than
> for consistency. If he saw two truths that
> seemed to contradict each other, he would take
> the two truths and contradiction along with
> them. His spiritual sight is stereoscopic, like his
> physical sight: he sees two different pictures at
> once and yet sees all the better for that. Thus,
> he has always believed that there was such a
> thing as fate, but such a thing as free will also.
> Thus, he believes that children were indeed the
> kingdom of heaven, but nevertheless ought to
> be obedient to the kingdom of earth. He
> admired youth because it was young and age
> because it was not. It is exactly this balance of
> apparent contradictions that has been the whole
> buoyancy of the healthy man. The whole secret
> of mysticism is this: that man can understand
> everything by the help of what he does not
> understand. The morbid logician seeks to make
> everything lucid, and succeeds in making eve-
> rything mysterious. The mystic allows one

thing to be mysterious, and everything else becomes lucid.[6]

Abandoning intellectual pride, and allowing the 'mysterious' to enter into one's worldview, demands real humility. Chesterton was, in some sense, the personification of humility. He received life and reality as pure gift, never grasping at it, or seeking to have his intellect dominate it, or even to understand it fully. He did, however, want people to acknowledge the marvel and majesty of their own lives, and not to become overserious, but rather to accept with child-like delight and pleasure the many gifts bestowed on them by God.

Taking oneself and the things in one's life too seriously [said Chesterton] constitutes a false religion in which we forget the great commandment: You shall love the Lord your God with all your heart, with all your soul, and with all your mind. In enjoying our God-given pleasures we are loving God, in letting other things destroy that enjoyment we are putting those things before God.[7]

In the writings of Chesterton there is what appears to be a near compulsion to communicate the remarkable height and depth and length and breadth of his vision. A.L. Maycock writes:

There was always in Chesterton an intense, a passionate desire to be understood. He constantly insisted that truth, in whatever form it is apprehended, should be a public possession. If a man has anything of value to say, it is his duty to say it and go on saying it as clearly and publicly as possible. That is one of Chesterton's essential characteristics as a writer. He taught. He explained. He taught men to see and understand things that they had never seen or understood before. We do not always recognize that

> he had all the gifts of a great teacher—lucidity,
> patience, a never failing freshness and originality
> of mind, a total absence of pomposity or self-
> importance, and, above all, an intense concern
> with the importance of what he had to say.[8]

As a teacher, as a visionary, Chesterton was never
condescending towards his readers or his listeners,
educated or un-educated. A statement such as the
following from Friedrich Nietzsche's *Thus Spake Zarathustra* would have been anathema to him: 'Life is a
well of joy; but where the rabble drinks too, all wells
are poisoned.'[9] Instinctively contradicting Nietzsche,
and expressed again and again in his work, is Chesterton's fundamental respect for ordinary humanity.
Chesterton believed in the common man not because
he was common but because, within each human
being, he recognized a being made in the image and
likeness of God. It was both the ordinary and extraordinary facts of human life he felt called to defend
against the insidious philosophy of nihilism.

> It is right that men should have houses, right
> that they should have land, right that they
> should have laws to protect the land; but all
> these things are only machinery to make leisure
> for the labouring soul. The house is only a stage
> set up by stage carpenters for the acting of what
> Mr. J. B. Yeats has called 'the drama of the
> home.' All the most dramatic things happen at
> home, from being born to being dead. What a
> man thinks about these things is his life; and to
> substitute for them a bustle of electioneering
> and legislation is to wander about among
> screens and pulleys on the wrong side of paste-
> board scenery; and never to act the play. And

that play is always a miracle play; and the name of its hero is Everyman.[10]

Chesterton campaigned against anything that crushed the human spirit, or which reduced human beings to mere cogs in a machine, or which negated utterly the spirit of fun and freedom. He wrote:

Employers are willing that workmen should have exercise, as it may help them do more work. They are even willing that workmen should have leisure; for the more intelligent capitalists can see that this also really means that they can do more work. But they are not in any way willing that workmen should have fun; for fun only increases the happiness and not the utility of the worker. Fun is freedom; and in that sense is an end in itself. It concerns the man not as a worker but as a citizen, or even as a soul; and the soul in that sense is an end in itself. That a man shall have a reasonable amount of comedy and poetry and even fantasy in his life is part of his spiritual health, which is for the service of God; and not merely for his mechanical health, which is now bound to the service of man. The very test adopted has all the servile implication; the test of what we can get out of him, instead of the test of what he can get out of life.[11]

As a disciple of truth, Chesterton opposed many of the popular assumptions of his day, assumptions which he knew would prove treacherous to human dignity. His life's work was a rally against the confinement of thought prevailing at that time, and still prevailing today. One assumption which Chesterton adamantly opposed was the notion of human existence as a mere byproduct of nature and not as something loved into being by an all-powerful Creator. On the impact which a certain kind of scientism has on our thinking today, Quentin Lauer remarks:

> There can be no question that the present century has seen more dramatic and extensive advances in sciences of nature than have the millennia that preceded it. There can be no question either, however, that the result of trying to understand the human spirit as more than a product of nature has been an enormous falsification of that spirit. The focus of all of Chesterton's output- literary criticism, poetry, biographies, novels, detective stories, the endless stream of essays, social, political, moral, religious- had but one ultimate end in view: to bring human beings to an ever-greater realization of the marvel of being human, a realization that was blocked in his day by the 'heresy' of seeing human beings as simply the product of nature.[12]

Developing further this view of G. K. Chesterton as visionary author, Arthur F. Thorn writes:

> We grow up in our feverish, artificial civilization, believing that the real, satisfying things are complex and difficult to obtain. Our lives become unnaturally stressed and tormented by the pitiless and incessant struggle for social conditions which are, at best, second-rate and ultimately disappointing. G. K. Chesterton would restore the primitive joys of wonder and childlike delight in simple things. His ideal is the real, not the merely impossible. Unlike most would-be saviours of the race, he seeks not to merge a new humanity into a brand new glitter- ing civilization. He would have us awaken once more to the ancient mysteries and eternal truths. He would have us turn back in order to progress.

Science makes us proud, but it does not make us happy. Efficiency makes us slaves—we have forgotten the truth about freedom. Success is our narcotic deity, and weans more men into despair than failure; for, as G. K. C. has said, 'Nothing fails like Success.' We have yet to rediscover the spiritual health that comes with a clear recognition of the part that life cannot be great until it is lived madly and wildly. We have to learn all over again that grass really is green, and the sky, at times, very blue indeed.[13]

Chesterton confronts the audacious assumptions of nihilism with the wild hope of Christianity. For Chesterton, this is not merely one lens among many with which to view the world. It is a putting aside of all 'lenses' in order to behold the gift of existence. It is not a detached viewing either. It is an engaged encounter with reality. It is answering the call to wonder. This vision Chesterton wanted to communicate to others not so much because it was wonderfully engaging, but because he believed it to be true, and because, more than any other path or vision, it affirmed the human being in all his joys and sorrows:

> Joy, which was the small publicity of the pagan, is the gigantic secret of the Christian ... The tremendous figure which fills the Gospels towers in this respect, as in every other, above all thinkers who ever thought themselves tall. His pathos was natural, almost casual. The Stoics, ancient and modern, were proud of concealing their tears. He never concealed His tears; He showed them plainly on his open face at any daily sight; such as the far sigh of His native city ... He never restrained his anger. He flung furniture down the front steps of the Temple, and asked men how they expected to

escape the damnation of Hell. Yet He restrained something ... There was some one thing that was too great for God to show us when He walked upon our earth; and I have sometimes fancied that it was His mirth.[14]

The infinite tenderness of God, manifest in the statement of Christ that every hair of our head is counted, is something Chesterton loved to contemplate. In *What's Wrong With The World*, he compares the whole of civilization with the red hair of a small child:

> I begin with a little girl's hair. That I know is a good thing at any rate. Whatever else is evil, the pride of a good mother in the beauty of her daughter is good. It is one of those adamantine tendernesses which are the touchstones of every age and race. If other things are against it, other things must go down. If landlords and laws and sciences are against it, landlords and laws and sciences must go down. With the red hair of one she-urchin in the gutter I will set fire to all modern civilization.

> Because a girl should have long hair, she should have clean hair; because she should have clean hair, she should not have an unclean home; because she should not have an unclean home, she should have a free and leisured mother; because she should have a free mother, she should not have an usurious landlord; because there should not be an usurious landlord, there should be a redistribution of property; because there should be a redistribution of property, there shall be a revolution.

> That little urchin with the gold-red hair, whom I have just watched toddling past my house, she shall not be lopped and lamed and altered; her

hair shall not be cut short like a convict's; no, all the kingdoms of the earth shall be hacked about and mutilated to suit her. She is the human and sacred image; all around her the social fabric shall sway and split and fall; the pillars of society shall be shaken, and the roofs of ages come rushing down, and not one hair of her head shall be harmed.[15]

In venturing to grasp Chesterton's perspective, it is worth noting the enormous significance he bestows on a little girl's hair, and how it literally outweighs in a sense all that civilization has to offer. The statement does not appear logical, it is true, but departing from human logic does not make Chesterton, in any way, illogical. It simply makes him theological. Here, as elsewhere, he is continually pointing to truths greater than himself and certainly greater than his own ability to comprehend them. There is an enormous seriousness in what he is attempting to say, but the liberating grace of the Christian imagination permits him to speak not only with daring but also with a saving lightness of touch and with great good humor. He writes:

The imagination dares to take the risks, it dares to have fun, dares to play, dares to 'waste time', dares to engage in nonsense. The Christian imagination can dare because it understands in its very depths that things are not as they seem — that the first shall be last, that the smallest shall be the greatest, that the proud shall be humbled, that the little child shall lead them all. The Christian imagination knows already that the solemn tomes of academe can be as nonsensical as the rhymes of a Pobble in the Gromboolian Plain. For the Christian imagination contains a

measure of that divine mirth that is at once the
patron of the arts and the preventer of madness.[16]

Every time an individual steps into play, the innocence, perspective, and glory of a child are reclaimed.
Sad to say, however, this imaginative vision of reality
and sense of wonder have, to a great extent, been lost
in our time. It is imperative, therefore, Chesterton
contends, to regain our sense of wonder. 'At the back
of our brains, so to speak, there was a forgotten blaze
or burst of astonishment at our own existence. The
object of the artistic and spiritual life was to dig for this
submerged sunrise of wonder'.[17]

## II. The Imagination Lost

Chesterton laments again and again at modernity's
treatment of the imagination. The Victorians, he tells
us, 'had a very real and even childlike wonder at things
like the steam-engine or the telephone considered as
toys.'[18] But much of that has been lost in modern times.
With the development of science, the authority of
science has greatly increased while the magic of fairy
tales has greatly diminished. That may not seem like
a great tragedy to many people today, but to Chesterton and to his friend Tolkien, this was indeed a
tragedy. For them the fantasy which is expressed in
fairy tales does not represent any kind of escape from
reality. On the contrary. Tolkien, in his essay *On
Fairy-Stories*, warns of the dangers which will inevitably threaten us if our human imagination no longer
draws on the springs of fantasy. We will become blind
to the wonder of the world around us. He writes:

Before we reach such states we need recovery. We
should look at green again, and be startled anew (but
not blinded) by blue and yellow and red. We should

meet the centaur and the dragon, and then perhaps suddenly behold, like the ancient shepherds, sheep, and dogs, and horses- and wolves. This recovery fairy-stories help us to make. In that sense only a taste for them may make us, or keep us, childish.[19]

Once vision is restored, one is able to have a firm and authentic grasp on reality, not only seeing objects clearly in their true essence, but beginning to perceive them *transcendentally*. This is the way Chesterton learned to view all things. He was never satisfied to see something or someone just as they were or appeared to be at this moment *empirically;* rather he saw them also in their transcendent reality, as what they might become. Jacques Maritain speaks of this in *Art and Scholasticism:*

> A similar antimony is implicit in all things which (like the mind and art) touch the transcendental order and are realized either in the state in God or 'by participation' in created subjects. As they tend (with an ineffective tendency which is none the less real) to the fullness of their essence considered in itself (transcendentally) and in its pure formal line, so they tend to surpass themselves, to cross the boundaries of their essence considered in a created subject (with the specific determinants there appropriate to it) and in so doing to escape from their condition of existence.[20]

This escape from the 'condition of existence' does not leave the observer behind but rather becomes an invitation to transcendence. It is a way of perceiving things not only as they are but as pointing beyond themselves. An awareness of creation's intrinsic potency allows one to be receptive, not only to transcendence, but to our ultimate end in God. The use of imagination, in this sense, becomes an expansion of reality rather than an escape from reality. Tolkien writes as follows regarding this question:

> Fantasy is made out of the Primary World, but a good craftsman loves his material and has a knowledge and a feeling for clay, stone and wood which only the art of making can give. By the forging of Gram cold iron was revealed; by the making of Pegasus horses were ennobled; in the Trees of the Sun and Moon root and stock, flower and fruit are manifested in glory ... For the story-maker who allows himself to be 'free with' Nature can be her lover not her slave. It is in fairy-stories that I first divined the potency of the words and the wonder of the things, such as stone, and wood, and iron; tree and grass; house and fire; bread and wine.[21]

Chesterton likewise rings the changes on the subject:

> I do not think there is anyone who takes quite such a fierce pleasure in things being themselves as I do. The startling wetness of water excites and intoxicates me: the fieriness of fire, the steeliness of steel, the unutterable muddiness of mud. It is just the same with people ... When we call a man 'manly' or a woman 'womanly' we touch the deepest philosophy.[22]

In his writings Chesterton was as much concerned with the application of our imaginative powers as he was with the application of reason. Worried about the effect of the contemporary world's treatment of the imagination, Chesterton sought to nourish a fidelity to the imagination, defending it against disparaging notions. He writes:

There is a notion adrift everywhere that imagination, especially mystical imagination, is dangerous to a man's mental balance ... Imagination does not breed insanity. Exactly what does breed insanity is reason. Poets do not go mad; but chess-players do. Mathematicians go mad, and cashiers; but creative artists very seldom. I am not, as will be seen, in any sense attacking logic; I only say that this danger does lie in logic, not in imagination ... The general fact is simple. Poetry is sane because it floats easily in an infinite sea; reason seeks to cross the infinite sea, and so make it finite ... The poet only asks to get his head into the heavens. It is the logician who seeks to get the heavens into his head. And it is his head that splits ... The madman is not the man who has lost his reason. The madman is the man who has lost everything except his reason.[23]

Is it possible that, at a certain point, Friedrich Nietzsche was one of those who 'lost everything except his reason'? And was that a factor perhaps in his mental collapse toward the end of his life? Speaking about philosophies he considers distorted, Chesterton writes:

I can see the inevitable smash of the philosophies of Schopenhauer and Tolstoy, Nietzsche and Shaw, as clearly as an inevitable railway smash could be seen from a balloon. They are all on the road to the emptiness of the asylum. For madness may be defined as using mental activity so as to reach mental helplessness; and they have nearly reached it.[24]

Modernity, for the most part, disregards the imaginative perspective as childish fantasy, a kind of irrespon-

sible play, for the same reason it disregards religion.
But Chesterton responds:

> It is not only possible to say a great deal in praise
> of play; it is really possible to say the highest
> things in praise of it. It might reasonably be
> maintained that the true object of all human life
> is play. Earth is a task garden; heaven is a
> playground. To be at least in such secure inno-
> cence that one can juggle with the universe and
> the stars, to be so good that one can treat every-
> thing as a joke—that may be, perhaps, the real
> end and final holiday of human souls. When we
> are really holy we may regard the universe as a
> lark ... that extreme degree of holiness which I
> have postulated as a necessary preliminary to
> such indulgence in the higher frivolity.[25]

Chesterton argued that it is the desire of every human
being, not only artists, to experience the wild and
unexpected world of the imagination. He writes:

> To the quietest human being, seated in the
> quietest house, there will sometimes come a
> sudden and unmeaning hunger for the possibil-
> ities or impossibilities of things; he will abruptly
> wonder whether the teapot may not suddenly
> begin to pour out honey or sea-water, the clock
> to point to all hours of the day at once, the
> candle to burn green or crimson, the door to
> open upon a lake or a potato-field instead of a
> London street.[26]

Chesterton vehemently criticized those who viewed
imagination as no more than the slave of idle fantasy,
something misleading, obscuring and deceitful. He
wrote:

The worst heresy ... is that the child is concerned only with make-believe. For this is interpreted in the sense, at once sentimental and skeptical, that there is not much difference between make-believe and belief. But the real child does not confuse fact and fiction. He simply likes fiction. He acts it because he cannot yet write it or even read it; but he never allows his moral sanity to be clouded by it. To him no two things could possibly be more contrary than playing at robbers and stealing sweets.[27]

As pointed out earlier, Chesterton's concern for the imagination is not solely grounded in the arts. The imagination plays a vital spiritual and theological role. On this point Dale Ahlquist writes:

The purpose of the imagination is to make us more like God ... That really is the purpose of the imagination. To make us more like God. After all, our imagination is a gift from God. It is perhaps one of the greatest gifts God has given us. It not only separates us from the beasts, it allows us to create new worlds of our own. Our imagination gives us a kind of omnipotence. There is almost nothing that we cannot do within the infinity of our minds. The Creator has made us in His own image. That is, he has made us creators. Our creativity is re-creation. And yes, it is recreation as well. It is restorative and rejuvenating. It is a pleasure. It is peace. It is a gift that we have abused, but perhaps even worse, it is a gift we have left unused.[28]

And again:

Just as we cannot lose our imagination, neither can we lose our reason. Reason and Imagination must go together. Our mental and spiritual

health depends on keeping this balance. We
must have an imaginative use of reason, and
reasonable use of imagination. Without reason,
the imagination merely runs wild and goes to
weeds. Chesterton says, 'Imagination is a thing
of clear images, and the more a thing becomes
vague the less imaginative it is. Similarly, the
more a thing becomes wild and lawless the less
imaginative it is.'[29]

Chesterton calls for a retrieval of wonder through an
authentic use of the imagination. He declares that 'the
world will never starve for want of wonders; but only
for want of wonder.'[30] When we do not engage our
imagination to perceive reality we no longer live with
a proper sense of perspective. We lose contact with the
child's sense of wonder. Chesterton writes:

There is something mysterious and perhaps
more than mortal about the power and call of
imagination. I do not think this early experience
[of childhood] has been quite rightly understood, even by those modern writers who have
written the most charming and fanciful studies
of childhood.[31]

Chesterton points to the child, or to the child's perspective, as the key to the recovery of that imaginative
grace, that creative innocence, so much ignored or
negated by the fashionable philosophies of our age.

## III. The Child as Guide to the Recovery of the Imagination

For Chesterton the child is indeed the one in possession of a truly fundamental wisdom. In *The Common
Man* he declares 'a child has a very sound sense of
wonder at what is really wonderful; and has by no

means merely a vulgar or varnished taste in what is conventionally beautiful ... Children are not snobs in art any more than in morals. And if they often have also a pleasure in things that are really "pretty" ... it is simply because there is a perfectly legitimate place in art for what is pretty.'[32] A child lives in the light of day. The thinkers of our age, in contrast, according to Chesterton, often live under the shadow of confused or distorted thinking. And that is why Chesterton, in his work, invites us all to step into the light of things as they are. He stands at the edge of the cave, as it were, and beckons us out into the open. We are to leave behind us the grim, mistaken thoughts which have held us prisoner for so long, and become, as the Gospel advises, children again. Of Chesterton the man and the teacher, K. Dwarakanath writes:

> He was a laughing philosopher who never outgrew that spontaneous and child-like sense of wonder and mystery in all things down from the starry sky to the small blades of grass under his feet. It was not the rainbow alone that made his heart leap up in wonder, but each and everything which had the glow of life in it. Indeed, the Wordsworthian paradox 'The child is the father of the man' could get a spirited and vital vindication in the personal life of G. K. Chesterton. The world was a fairyland to him where he saw miracle in truth and truth in miracle, and he sang the glory of the everlasting life that teems in the sun and the streams, hills and dales, men, women and children, friends, admirers and adversaries.[33]

That 'the child is the father of the man' is a truth also manifest in the life and work of Charles Dickens, an author hugely admired by Chesterton. Certain of the

observations Dickens makes about the young heroes in
*A Child's Dream of a Star* are, almost certainly, an evoca-
tion of his own sense of wonder as a child. Concerning
the two young people he writes: 'They wondered at the
beauty of flowers; they wondered at the height and
blueness of the sky; they wondered at the depth of the
bright water; they wondered at the goodness and power
of God who made the lovely world.'[34]

For Chesterton a child's 'take on things' is almost
always the wisest. In *Lunacy and Letters*, he writes:

> The child has no need of nonsense: to him the
> whole universe is nonsensical in the noblest
> sense of that noble word. A tree is something
> top-heavy and fantastic, a donkey is as exciting
> as a dragon. All objects are seen through a great
> magnifying glass ... A child has innumerable
> points of inferiority ... but he has one real point
> of superiority. We are going forth continually
> to discover new aesthetic worlds, and last of all
> our conquests we have discovered this world
> of nonsense. But he has appreciated this world
> at a glance, and first glances are best.[35]

This is the wonderful world of childhood, and all the
magic that it possesses comes naturally to the child.
The adult, through an act of will, or of memory, or
through an act of the imagination, can also partake of
this magic, and recapture the vision, as Chesterton
does, through the lens of childhood:

> Did you ever hear a small boy complain of
> having to hang about a railway station and wait
> for a train? No; for to him to be inside a railway
> station is to be inside a cavern of wonder and a
> palace of poetical pleasures. Because to him the
> red light and the green light on the signal are
> like a new sun and a new moon. Because to him

when the wooden arm of the signal falls down suddenly, it is as if a great king had thrown down his staff as a signal started a shrieking tournament of trains. I myself am of little boys' habit in this matter.[36]

A child may get tired, but he never tires of reality. He is forever absorbed and engaged in the wonder of things as they are.

A child kicks his legs rhythmically through excess, not absence, of life. Because children have abounding vitality, because they are in spirit fierce and free, therefore they want things repeated and unchanged. They always say, 'Do it again'; and the grown-up person does it again until he is nearly dead.[37]

For adults to recover the sense of the miracle of life and recover the sense of fun in life, they need, according to Chesterton, to look to the child as a sort of guide. He writes:

> The child is, indeed, in these, and many other matters, the best guide. And in nothing is the child so righteously childlike, in nothing does he exhibit more accurately the sounder order of simplicity, than in the fact that he sees everything with a simple pleasure, even the complex things. The false type of naturalness harps always on the distinction between the natural and the artificial. The higher kind of naturalness ignores that distinction. To the child the tree and the lamp-post are as natural and as artificial as each other; or rather, neither of them are natural but both supernatural. For both are splendid and unexplained.[38]

That there is anything at all is to the child a marvel. The child apprehends the simple fact of existence with an instinctive wisdom no philosophy can ever provide.

This observation is one Chesterton makes in his great work on St Thomas Aquinas. And, in the same work, he makes the following splendid statement which can serve to bring our present reflections on the child as our best guide to the recovery of imagination to a conclusion:

> When a child looks out of the nursery window and sees anything, say the green lawn of the garden, what does he actually know; or does he know anything? ... A brilliant Victorian scientist delighted in declaring that the child does not see grass at all; but only a sort of green mist reflected in a tiny mirror of the human eye ... Men of another school answer that grass is a mere green impression on the mind; and the child can be sure of nothing except the mind ... St Thomas Aquinas, suddenly intervening in this nursery quarrel, says emphatically that the child is aware of *Ens*. Long before he knows that grass is grass, or self is self, he knows that something is something. Perhaps it would be best to say very emphatically (with a blow on the table). There *is* an Is.[39]

## Notes

1    G. K. Chesterton, *The Everlasting Man* (New York: Dodd, Mead & Company, 1942), 261–2.
2    G. K. Chesterton, *Orthodoxy* (New York: Dodd, Mead and Company, 1959), 46.
3    G. K. Chesterton, *The Thing; Why I Am a Catholic* (New York: Dodd, Mead & Co., 1930), 217.
4    G. K. Chesterton, *As I Was Saying* (New York: Books for Libraries Press, 1966), 185.
5    G. K. Chesterton, *The Illustrated London News*, 6 January 1906, in vol.27 of *The Collected Works of G. K. Chesterton*, ed. Lawrence J. Clipper (San Francisco: Ignatius Press), 98.

6   *Orthodoxy*, 48–9.

7   G. K. Chesterton, cited in Thomas C. Peters, *The Christian Imagination: G. K. Chesterton on the Arts* (San Francisco: Ignatius Press, 2000), 124.

8   A. L. Maycock (ed.), Introduction, G. K. Chesterton, *The Man Who Was Orthodox: A Selection from the Uncollected Works of G. K. Chesterton*, (London: Dennis Dobson, 1963), 14.

9   Friedrich Wilhelm Nietzsche, *Thus Spoke Zarathustra: A Book for Everyone and Nobody*, trans. Graham Parkes (New York: Oxford University Press, 2005), 83.

10  G. K. Chesterton, *Irish Impressions* (San Francisco: Ignatius Press, 2001), 187.

11  G. K. Chesterton, *What I Saw in America, The Collected Works of G. K. Chesterton*, vol.21, ed. Robert Royal (San Francisco: Ignatius Press, 1990), 147.

12  *Philosopher Without Portfolio*, 152.

13  Arthur F. Thorn, cited in Patrick Braybrooke, *Gilbert Keith Chesterton*, (Philadelphia: J.B Lippincott Company, 1922), x.

14  *Orthodoxy*, 298.

15  G. K. Chesterton, *What's Wrong with the World*, (New York: Dodd, Mead and Company, 1912), 356–7.

16  *The Christian Imagination*, 42.

17  *The Autobiography of G. K. Chesterton*, 90.

18  G. K. Chesterton, *Fancies Versus Fads* (London: Methuen and Company, 1923), 209.

19  J. R. R. Tolkien, *Tree and Leaf* (Boston: Houghton Mifflin Company 1965), 57.

20  Jacques Maritain, *Art and Scholasticism*, trans. James Scanlan (London: Sheed & Ward, 1930), 173.

21  *Tree and Leaf*, 59.

22  G. K.Chesterton, cited in Maisie Ward, *Gilbert Keith Chesterton* (Lanham: Rowman & Littlefield Publishers, 2006), 97.

23  *Orthodoxy*, 27–32.

24  *Orthodoxy*, 76.

25  *The Christian Imagination*, 124.

26  G. K. Chesterton, *The Defendant* (London: J.M. Dent & Sons, 1901), 125.

27  *The Autobiography of G. K. Chesterton*, 39.

28  Dale Ahlquist, 'G. K. Chesterton and the Use of the Imagination', *Dappled Things: a quarterly of ideas art and faith*,

http://dappledthings.org/90/g-k-chesterton-and-the-use-of-the-imagination/, (accessed 24 January, 2012).

29   *Ibid.*

30   *Tremendous Trifles*, 7.

31   G. K. Chesterton, *The Common Man* (London: Sheed & Ward, 1950), 56.

32   Ibid., 114.

33   *G. K. Chesterton: A Critical Study*, 233.

34   Charles Dickens, *A Child's Dream of a Star*. (Boston: Fields, Osgood & Co., 1871), 5.

35   *Lunacy and Letters*, 27.

36   G. K. Chesterton, 'On Running After One's Hat' (*All Things Considered*, 1908), *In Defense of Sanity: The Best Essays of G. K. Chesterton*, eds. Dale Ahlquist et al (San Francisco, Ignatius Press 2011), 22.

37   *Orthodoxy*, 108.

38   *Heretics*, 139.

39   *Saint Thomas Aquinas*, 204–6.

# CONCLUSION

HESTERTON'S THEOLOGY OF WONDER proclaims and explores the sacramental and sacred element in all that exists. He views the world like a child, but always *theologically*, finding himself again and again literally drenched in the wonder of existence.

Chesterton can hold up a pen, a glass, a stone, and can find in it the signature of God. In the multiplicity of things he perceives not a distant, pantheistic, or absent God, but an intimate friend, a God who has dared to give to humanity the gift of free-will. This decision of providence prompts Chesterton, as a theologian, to ponder deeply the marvelous peril of such a wild and extravagant gift.

Chesterton encounters within the drama of history the Incarnation, the Cross and the Resurrection. These events are staggering to the human mind. And since, inevitably, comprehension on the intellectual level will never be satisfactory, Chesterton always approaches these events with humility and gratitude.

Following in the tradition of Aquinas, Chesterton chooses to explore the puzzles and problems of creation with metaphysical insight and intuition. He is not afraid to confront head-on, therefore, the reality of evil in the world. To Chesterton this dark dimension of reality is as distinct and real as the many wonders he beholds within existence. But Chesterton never allows this knowledge of the reality of evil to negate all that is good in the world. One of the striking paradoxes of his life is that it was his very grappling with the phenomenon of evil—even in its diabolical form—

which, at one point compelled his mind not just to see the good but, in the end, to rely on it completely.

When, on one occasion, Chesterton was asked why he converted to Catholicism, he answered, 'So my sins could be forgiven.' For Chesterton, the forgiveness of sins offered by Christ to the sinner opened the door into a marvellous world of blessing, an unforeseen return to innocence and purity, a wholly unexpected grace.

Chesterton reproached many of his contemporaries for what they had allowed themselves to become. He knew the perils inherent in a misguided philosophy and how often the road to perdition was paved by errant thinking. One of the reasons which led to his conversion to the Catholic Church was the importance and primacy he gave to tradition. In this respect his path resembled that of John Henry Newman. Chesterton knew very well the importance of a philosophy anchored in tradition. As a modern commentator on secular affairs, he acted in some way almost in a magisterial capacity. By challenging and reprimanding the philosophies of modernity, Chesterton pointed a way back to the freshness and wisdom of ancient truths. He was, to steal a phrase of Teilhard de Chardin from another context, 'a pilgrim of the future, returning from a journey made entirely in the past.'

Chesterton's arrival at 'the root of sanity' marked the terminus of a long journey happily pursued along a metaphysical path, largely influenced by Aquinas. In his debate with philosophers such as Schopenhauer and Nietzsche, it was to the wisdom of Aquinas Chesterton looked again and again to offset anything he considered absurd or despairing. Chesterton never forgot what we find so often missing in modern philosophy, namely the knowledge of humanity's dependence upon God, our Creator. By emphasizing this doctrine, Chesterton sought to restore to our contemporary world that child-like sense of gratitude and wonder concerning existence, without which there is, in this world, no deep or lasting joy.

Truth does not go out of fashion, but philosophies quite often do. And if they are false philosophies, they can have, for as long as they last, dire consequences. Entire lives and generations can be ruined on the rocks of an errant philosophy. How is it, for example, that systematic genocide could be brought into existence? How is it that the past century became the bloodiest in human history? The answer lies in certain errant paths of thought pursued whole-heartedly by fallen humanity. When human beings fall into mistaken thinking, they quite often fall spectacularly. This Chesterton knew very well and understood. It is one of the reasons his writings are still relevant today. He grasped the paradoxical nature of human beings, understood that we are capable of both the greatest good and the greatest evil, and capable also of not just betraying ourselves and others, but of even betraying God to whom we owe the utmost fidelity.

Of the many belief systems Chesterton considered, Christianity was the only one which completely captured his mind and heart. He wrote:

> The more I considered Christianity, the more I found that while it had established a rule and order, the chief aim of that order was to give room for good things to run wild ... St Francis, in praising all good, could be a more shouting optimist than Walt Whitman. St Jerome, in denouncing all evil, could paint the world blacker than Schopenhauer.[1]

Catholicism, Chesterton found, answered the call of the wildest mystic as well as the challenge of the deepest thinker. It offered humanity a vision able somehow to embrace both finitude and transcendent desire, gradually transforming us, therefore, not into something other than ourselves, but into beings more truly ourselves. Catholicism alone, he believed, is capable of saving our world from the dreadful gloom of life-denying philosophies such as nihilism. By pointing out for us, at a time of great confusion, the wonderful sanity of the Gospel path, it is able to lead us back to the eternal truths of tradition and, at the same time, open us up to an entirely new and graced vision of the world around us.

In conclusion, it is perhaps appropriate to end with a text by Saint John Paul II on the subject of wonder, a text which might well have been written by G. K. Chesterton himself:

> [W]e need first of all to foster, in ourselves and in others, a contemplative outlook. Such an outlook arises from faith in the God of life, who has created every individual as a 'wonder' (cf. Ps 139:14). It is the outlook of those who see life in its deeper meaning, who grasp its utter gratuitousness, its beauty and its invitation to freedom and responsibility. It is the outlook of those who do not presume to take possession of reality but instead accept it as a gift, discovering in all things the reflection of the Creator and seeing in every person His living image. (cf. Gen 1:27; Ps 8:5)[2]

# Notes

1   *Orthodoxy*, 175–77.
2   Saint John Paul II, Encyclical Letter *Evangelium Vitae* (Washington, DC: United States Catholic Conference, 1995), 83.

Lightning Source UK Ltd.
Milton Keynes UK
UKOW04f0155060215

245769UK00001B/9/P